AF253358

# ALL THE LOVE

# WE CANNOT FEEL

**JAMES WATT**

# TABLE OF CONTENTS

# AN INTRODUCTION

~

Have you ever felt that this world belongs to every-one but you? That try as you might you don't really feel at home in your own skin? That was life for me in the years of my youth. Most people seemed able to relax and enjoy the company of others but I felt on the outside, alone. Living in a family of four brothers, two sisters and two live-in parents seems an automatic pass for the 'how to socialize class' … but not for this little black duck. There was a seven year gap between my closest sibling and what seemed like 77 years to get one parent's attention. I got used to taking care of myself.

There would eventually be someone whom I knew loved me. She would notice me – even occasionally listen to me.

Life did change … slowly. I was still quiet and anxious, but more sociable, even capable of relaxing at parties rather than panic at the approach of a stranger.

Then marriage and children brought more change. My firstborn came into the world accompanied by an explosion of love. Somehow it poured out of somewhere when I first took him into my arms. Where it came from was still a secret. I knew this son of mine belonged on the earth but his dad was still stuck somewhere between moments like this and times that threatened to suck the life from him.

Where did all that love come from? I didn't have it on tap and I didn't know how to access it when I most needed it. When the black dog of depression attacked, its savagery could come into me virtually unopposed. I would feel myself drowning again, lost in a tempest that bit and scrapped at the frayed edges of my shrunken heart.

When my eldest enrolled in university, it was the same tertiary institution I had enrolled in – not years ago but the same year. Not only were we going to travel together there, we would also be in the same class doing the same subject 'Relational Dynamics'. My wife (his mother) had been encouraging at least one of us to enrol. When news of both boys being in this same subject rolled in, we were all surprised. Matty and I were now part of a Masters counseling programme and our first subject was examining the good, bad and ugly in one's family of origin.

Had I been a half decent father? Would my son want to punch me in the face during class time or on the way home? Questions assailed, fears awakened deep within. I knew I had been a better dad than my own, but had I been good enough? I was too often angry with the kids, still subject to forces that had remained in the dark for many years.

You see my life has been full of secrets – to the left and to the right. And for now I am going to become a little more secretive and discontinue this story in first person. Some things need to forever remain at least a little secret.

# LITTLE TIM & CO

## *The Family, Dad, Mum, An Aside, The Kids*

~

Tiny little Tim was the pleasant surprise of his family. He snuck up on his mum and dad. Liz and Bill were on the verge of menopausal years, neither one really expecting a late entry on the roster. The family swayed between rugby and basketball as their sport of choice and it was not mum's ambition to supply the full set of forwards that her hubby sometimes dreamed of. They were a suburban middle class couple already enjoying the presence of six children and number seven could mean an all male basketball starting five. They also had two girls and though all three enthused over basketball as much as the boys, Liz was glad to have some support of a more feminine nature. Josephine was the eldest in the family and she shared some of Liz's matriarchal qualities along with some feminine flair. They also formed a beach volleyball team with number two daughter coming in off the bench when needed.

The Wests did not use contraception. They took the teaching of the Catholic Church seriously and understood there was a biblical command to fill the earth. They simply thought that six children was a full house and sufficient to fulfill the religious obligation to flood the Australian landscape with Catholic kids. They enjoyed the means of production together as much as any full blooded couple in their prime and they even loved each other as well. However when the doctor confirmed the pregnancy, Liz could not look forward to telling anyone in the same way she had announced the previous six. Bill might start thinking about that set of eight rugby forwards again. Why couldn't he accept that League (which only has six forwards) was an acceptable form of the game? Surely he would feel the weight of another mouth eating into the food budget as well as everything else that occupied their full lives. Thoughts of sleepless nights, soaking nappies and second-hand clothes for nine all threatened Liz's peace. On top of that her already overstretched emotional capacity had another challenge developing.

Anxiety slowly crept up Liz's spinal cord and entered her cerebral cortex. The little fella in her belly began to pick up on negative feelings, some doubts as to whether or not his conception was a good idea. He was not yet conscious of this of course but something dark began to form in his small shape. Thankfully abortion was not an option for this family's religious fraternity, so he was safe at that level, but he was not protected from maternal resentments growing into chemical reactions around his developing form. It's not only food that travels down that umbilical connection between mother and son. There are also physical side effects of maternal concern and worry. It wasn't all bad because mum was not entirely fearful of number seven. Memories of the wonder and beauty of a newborn brought comfort to both her and her little Tim as he grew within.

Indeed it wasn't all bad for Tim because his internal habitat was really quite cosy. The walls of his room were soft, flexible and he felt quite snug a lot of the time. He was able to lie around all day, his pleasure inputs and outputs automatically fulfilled by his female carer. Sounds like paradise for many an Australian male. In the land of the long weekend, a comfortable lounge area in the backyard might still be considered a constitutional right. The question for our young hero is how long will this laid back existence last when he journeys beyond? What waits outside his current chamber? What discoveries lie on the other side of that wall? There are encouraging signs in the family as well as discouraging ones thus far.

## The Family

There is a mixed family reception awaiting the arrival of the latest West. The umbilical cord is passing on loads of healthy nutrition accompanied by an increasing amount of negative emotions with most of the family contributing. Bill was on the verge of a promotion at the bank, which would help the cash flow for bubba but would he have enough time to get the increased load done at work and at home? Liz expanded her worry base with Bill's concerns increasingly becoming hers too. Eldest Josephine was turning 15 the same day as the predicted arrival of the new sibling. What would this do to her standing in the family, no longer the centre of attention on her special day? Albert the eldest son at 14 thought the dethroning of Josephine would be awesome, so he was about the only one totally on Tim's side. Twelve-yea-rold Harold was happy to have another sibling under him who would increase the number of indentured slaves from which he could demand service. His intentions probably couldn't make their malicious way down the umbilical cord because they were largely secret, but with Harold, many things are possible. In light of this, two-years-younger Brendan specialized as the invisible man, so he saw number seven as simply that – another statistic to be avoided just as much as he avoided number three, Harold, whenever possible. Bob stood at number five child and just the thought of another competitor for parental affection was enough to activate his fighting spirit against the latest upstart. Finally young Geraldine thought that the stats were in favour of another female, so her focus remained on preparing for a baby in her image, a little sister who would wear precious dresses now too small for herself.

# Dad

Bill worked in a bank. He was on the verge of being promoted to manage the personal loan section of the city branch he toiled in. Supporting six kids and the exhausted family worker (yes that's Liz) had not been easy. He was hoping the promotion would come in time to purchase some new baby items.

So he looked for the pram on the weekend to see if it could hold up one more time. He called out at the back door "Hey everyone! Has anyone seen the pram lately, I'm sure I stored it in the garage?" No one answers. Liz relays it further into the house.

Harold thinks it's a little early to be worried about a pram when there are so many months to go. He calls out "It's OK dad – Tom O'Reilly borrowed it for his mum to have a look at. She wanted to check out a pram that had survived six kids."

"Well go and tell Tom O'Reilly that your dad wants to do exactly the same thing." A fatherly pause, then "Hang on, why do you know so much about it?"

"Mum wasn't home on Thursday arvo when Tom came over, so I used a little initiative and showed him where it was. I forgot to tell mum about it."

"OK then off you go – Dianne should have finished her analysis by now."

Harold had lent the pram to a mate up the road with a similar predilection for terrorizing siblings. He had regularly called on it as a downhill racer into which younger relatives were conscripted as pilots. Their lack of training as pilots didn't stop the 'Hill Programme'. The mate had siblings that could still fit into the pilot's seat and Harold hadn't reckoned on dad being so organized. The return of the perambulator only confirmed the reality that four boys and two girls had fully utilized that vessel.

Bill told Liz "This pram is stuffed". Another fatherly pause, "Sometimes I feel a bit the same."

Liz replied, "Only sometimes hon? Maybe you need to get another job then you can feel like that all the time." Bill knew Liz really was a trooper keeping the squad in line most of the time. She was more wasted than him and he smiled at her little joke. The pram had sat unused for seven years in the garage (well, almost unused, given Harold's little secret) but the thought of a seven-year holiday manifested a touch of pram envy. It had been left to itself - nothing demanded of it. If only Bill could have some of that.

Not today however, because there were clothes in the garage, lots of old clothes needing to be retrieved and evaluated before the arrival. Their hand-me-down clothing was big on quantity but nowhere near sufficient quality. Air vents were visible in the boys' shorts and shirts and Bill remembered how they could appear without any warning. All the boys had been hyperactive both inside and outside the cot so the chances of a quiet one who didn't hyperactivate regularly was perhaps 100 to one. Bill had never backed a winner at those odds.

Winter would be in full swing when the bub arrived on the outside so more clothes would be needed. Bill was pretty sure it was another boy because Liz's breath matured during the male pregnancies and at the moment it was blue cheese eau de parfum. Her mid term breath prevented the concept of future lovemaking ever being possible, let alone another male conception being achieved.

## Mum

Liz's Catholic Irish family, the O'Donovans, emigrated to the land of Oz before her birth. Note that Catholic appears before Irish in the order of importance. She had never seen the green green grass of County Cork but she sure as hell knew the difference between an English Protestant and an Irish Catholic. That demarcation line was just as real in the distant prison that housed Irish ancestors as it was in the land of leprechauns. Her family were definitely on one side, the only right side of course. Suspicions arose around any crossing of unseen but clear boundaries of ethnicity and faith. Many a time Liz's mother said, "Whatever you do with your life Liz, don't ever bring one of those Protestant bastards home. You can't trust them, not even one!"

"Yes mum." Liz agreed with her every time but she

hadn't yet met the man who would expand this world view. Bill was not English but he was a Protestant and that was enough to curl the hair on the back of Liz's neck when they first met in the Irish pub in Surry Hills. It was then inconceivable to the O'Donovan world view that such a person should even be inside an Irish pub let alone talking to her. Religion somehow arose in their conversation.

"Hey I don't go to church every Sunday, just when I feel I need to."

Liz replied, "What do you mean that you don't go every Sunday? Are you fond of committing mortal sins then?"

"Mortal sins – what are you talking about? I'm not fond of many sins, what's a mortal one?"

"You don't know? What are you doing drinking here then?"

"I like the Guinness on tap, is that a mortal sin?"

"Well no. What church do you go to?

"Presbyterian."

"Presbyterian! Not Catholic! And you like Guinness and Irish pubs and Irish girls?" Liz had too much going on in her head. The impossible had already occurred twice tonight. This guy she likes goes to a Protestant church and he likes drinking Guinness in an Irish pub. Too much information.

Bill takes over the role of interrogator. "Yes I like all three Irish institutions just like you said. Why is that so hard to believe?" Silence from Liz … ongoing silence from Liz.

"Have you ever met many people who aren't Catholic, Liz?" This question stretched Liz's cranial capacity even further but after another exemplary demonstration of Bill's patience she was able to respond. "Not many really and those that I have met were not like you."

"How am I different?"

"Well you're patient for one thing and you aren't bashing up my brother for another. Most of them called us tykes and threw rocks as well, so I guess my protestant experience is mainly on the dark side."

Also she didn't know if it was a plus or a minus that he only visited his Presbyterian church on occasion. They had been getting on famously till religion came up. It's not good form to speak about such things on an Aussie first date which is what their interaction had become, but neither one knew how it had actually come up. Come up it had though. It was on the playing field and it could not be hidden away. Nor could the fact that each individual was worth spending time with, despite the fact that both were on the wrong side of the demarcation line.

Mrs O'Donovan continued to make that line clear when Liz eventually took him home for a visit. "What the hell have I been telling you all these 23 years girl! Don't bring home a Protestant bastard and what do you do? Bring home a Protestant bastard!"

"He isn't a bastard, he's only Protestant"

"The two things are the same girl."

"Well what if he became a Catholic?"

"That would make him a Catholic bastard. I guess there are one or two of them you know."

"OK, then I won't bring him home anymore."

"And you won't see him anymore."

"Perhaps I won't see you anymore, mum. For now, he stays in my life and that's that." Mrs O'Donovan wondered where her daughter got her strong opinions from.

The fact that Bill wasn't overly religious played in Romeo and Juliet's favour eventually, because he was prepared to surrender his Presbyterian citizenship and sign up Roman Catholic Church Irish style. He would never be Catholic in the eyes of his Irish in-laws but his decision had always touched Liz deep down and was one of the many reasons she loved him. He had passed her cross-examination on their first date, now Liz was the one likely to face a cross-examination. If the new bub didn't have the West jaw one could begin to wonder what was going on. It was the family resemblance that irrefutably declared the arrival of another West. Bill had a strong jaw and so did all his kids thus far, but would number seven follow the tradition or would he look more like the gentleman who Liz had met on the girls' night months ago.

Drunken decisions can lead to drunken liaisons. She was not the only girl that night to wish they had not played all those shot games while hanging out with whoever those guys were. There's nothing wrong with having a good drink in Catholic World, but other acts associated with loosened morals may be viewed more seriously, and Liz had much on her mind. Did we really go that far? Why do I still fraternize with those old girlfriends? Is that a real memory or guilt by association?

## An Aside

Remember Tim is picking up some of this anxiety because the umbilical system doesn't only transport nutrition it also imports negative emotions in chemical form. There was a regular invasion taking place via that little aqueduct and the impression began to form in little Tim that rather than being joyfully received as the final male on the starting basketball team, he would be seen as the benchman that no one really wanted.

## The Kids

Meanwhile Albert was more interested in the girl across the street than Tim. She had worn a two-piece swimsuit for the first time last summer and Albert still had that image in his mind most of the time as he cooked up ways of winning her heart. Summer itself hadn't been as hot as usual but hot is how Albert remembers it because his temperature went up every time he saw her.

Harold and Brendan obsessed over the upcoming

rugby season so there was only the occasional malicious notion about Tim that Harold put aside for future reference. Brendan was aiming for best and fairest again and he didn't have much time or care for anything but remaining fit and safe from any of Harold's unforeseen attacks. Bob pondered on ways to improve his dance moves, which always got smiles from mum. Geraldine had never seen mum with the bumpy tum and she was more excited than anyone else about a little sister that was on the way. Dad had said they didn't know if it was going to be a boy or a girl but Geraldine had a feminine instinct that was only occasionally wrong. *She was going to be a girl.*

# THE ARRIVAL

~

The West family had moved into a young suburb where urban development had managed to preserve a few of the large trees that once dominated the area. Gums had been the predominant variety but some trees had immigrated and knew how to survive. The West's land plot accommodated a middle-aged liquid amber tree and its leaves reflected the cycle of life, death and resurrection through the changing colours. The bright red autumn leaves had long blackened and been returned to the soil on the day that little Tim arrived.

The boys were practicing their rugby skills in the backyard after school when a misdirected kick hit the composting gardener fair and square in the belly. Yes, Liz was the aforementioned gardener. It may have been the hidden beginning of Tim's football career but it was certainly the beginning of Liz's contractions. Brendan had attempted a speculator, which went up in the air, not too high, but high enough to hit the bump on mum's tum on its downward trajectory. Mum had only just leaned back to take a breather when the ball's impact initiated a series of rapidly increasing groans that Brendan interpreted as attempted murder. He was too young to know it couldn't be more than manslaughter. All he could see was 'mumslaughter'. Brendan joined in the groaning. Dad raced outside to see what was happening.

"Liz, is it the time?"

"What does it sound like honey?" Answering a question with a question was part of mum's communicatory arsenal.

And more urgently Brendan cried out, "Is it time to die?!"

"No Brendan, mum is simply getting ready to deliver our latest West," says dad.

"You mean she is going to be OK?"

"Yes of course she is. This is what it's like when a new baby comes into the world."

The girls had come outside and caught that last line. Geraldine ventured, "Looks like a lotta trouble to me dad."

"No it's not honey ... well it's not easy but when the head's out ..."

Mum protests, "Now is not the time for sex education Bill! Now is the time for hospital!"

Bill had been coming home early from work all week to be here in case of this and now he had to cut the conversation and move into action. Liz could feel another serious contraction coming and it hadn't been much time since the previous ones. All the West births, bar one, had roughly approximated to the medical predictions given. A couple of bubs had been induced with no rushing around at all. Bill recalled five times Liz was dropped off and taken to a place where maternal screams were unlikely to be heard. Hospitals used to prevent any paternal participation in the actual birth. The only male hazard was sitting in the hospital waiting room, trying not to breathe in smoke from anxiety-ridden hubbies.

There was one occasion when Bill became actively involved – Harold's birth. Like Tim, he was in a hurry to get out. Contractions started in the dead of night when they lived in a terrace close to the city. They didn't own four-wheeled transport. A taxi had been ordered ahead of time as contractions slowly increased and they waited patiently just like the two previous arrivals. Then suddenly the contractions came every few minutes and the taxi had still not arrived. Phone calls to the taxi company produced nothing but Liz was almost ready to introduce number three West to the outside world. Bill called on the help of their neighbours who owned a recently imported Ford Fairlane. It had more than enough room for the couple in the back while Don the driver occupied the bench seat up front. He was one serious car owner still weaning his own new baby and he took longer than the normal ten minutes to get to the hospital. Don could hear the urgency of Liz's yells on the increase as he reluctantly agreed to drive faster. However neither he nor

Bill were ready for Liz's scream as Harold's head was first sighted in the back of the Fairlane. It wasn't just one scream. With each increasingly urgent scream, more of the latest bub's head appeared, much to the concern of his befuddled father.

Don spoke up, "Can't you wait a little longer Liz?"

No reply from mum but dad enunciated, "We reached the point of no return at the traffic lights Don."

"We aren't going to make it then, like, to the hospital?"

"No Don, I just became a midwife, our baby boy is almost all here."

The final phase of delivery took place as Don parked the car at the emergency door, too late to save his back-seat from the biological consequences of a recently emerged newborn. Don was upset but Bill was relieved to have trained help concerned about assisting mum and son into the building.

Don's wife admired the heroism of all involved in this short trip to the hospital. However Don's number one priority in life was having his own pride and joy in pristine condition. His dedication to chrome and glory meant any relationship with 'those bloody neighbours' was over. He had the kind of faith in cars that was destined to be made famous on the Aussie TV show 'Kingswood Country' before a Kingswood even existed. (A Kingswood is a mid range Holden car venerated by many middle class Aussies.) Truly Don was a man before his time.

Now back at the scene of the current prenatal exit

strategy being employed by Tim. Bill was struck by the strength of Liz's last scream. It was just like the scream in the back of Don's car. His own car was smaller than Don's. He was driving with Liz occupying the entire back seat. There were no midwives, part-time or full-time, available in any seat of this car. He exceeded legal speed limits.

They arrived just in time for Liz to be rolled into the labour ward as Tim completed his entrance. Bill had been well prepared. A test trip had timed at nine minutes and 22 seconds. This trip took five minutes flat. Liz often commented on near-death experiences at dinner parties and they weren't referring to life at war. She would describe the intensity of her contractions during labour and the need for instant pain relief via intravenous drugs preventing imminent death. With Jo and Albert in charge at home and Liz hooked up to the vital pain relief, both parents could relax a bit. Non-smoker Bill didn't have to endure even one smoke cloud because of the hasty arrival. Whether Tim was rushing in response to the feel of the footy through mum's tum or not, it is true the call of the pigskin would one day play a major role in his life.

Tim West was born at 0432 on 31st July 1958 – fresh air for the boy at last. He breathed, he cried and he caught a glimpse of mum as he was whisked away to be cleaned up and placed in a sterile environment. His crib was nowhere near as cosy as the cave he had inhabited for months, so he cried some more and wondered where the comforting thump-thump had gone to. It was an independence day of sorts … too much independence for his age and a theme that would repeat itself later on in life.

Mum meanwhile was away with the birds, high on drugs, getting 14 stitches having undergone another near-death experience. She was only vaguely aware that Bill was going to view the latest West before she had a chance to.

The 'one evening stand', if that's what it was, had been with a man of Aryan origins, all blonde hair and blue eyes. The Wests were all combinations of dark brown and ginger accompanied by a Roger Ramjet jaw. (Cartoon pilot Ramjet had a jaw twice as big as Charlton Heston's i.e. BIG.) Would her darling babe resemble a member of the British Empire or a card-carrying member of the recently disempowered Third Reich?

Bill had gone home after the birth to make sure the kids were all set for school. He had been so concerned about Liz and home, he hadn't gone to the nursery to check on Tim before he left. Now he was back mid morning checking on Liz first and then telling her he was off to the nursery. Liz reassured herself that most babies look like Winston Churchill anyway but she still sweated on Bill's return. Her waiting time was lengthened by a nurse's bad aim. She had managed to place a pin not only through Tim's nappy but also through his wee foreskin. Did the nurse understand Tim was Catholic and think the damaged skin would soon be removed anyway?

Matron held dad up at the pass, "Mr West have you washed your hands?"

"At least once today."

"And when was that exactly?"

"Ah before breakfast."

"So are you hoping to finger feed some of your breakfast to your son?"

"Of course not."

"Off you go then, wash them and have a look at your face in the mirror too, you might consider giving that mug a makeover."

Bill obeyed and noticed his reflection was in desperate need of more waking up. Then he remembered to organize some flowers for Liz before returning to the nursery. Meanwhile a more competent nurse released the nappy pin and settled the beleaguered infant before any premature circumcision was reported. Tim was finally handed over to his father and Mr West proudly presented the brown-haired bub with the Ramjet chin to his relieved mother. Liz placed him on her breast and the rush of milk may have been a let down in technical terms but for little Tim it was a magic moment. He drank up and fell asleep in his mother's arms fully sated and mightily relieved that the circumcision ceremony had not been brought forward to today.

# YEAR ONE

*In life, not school*

~

Bank management heard another West had been added to the ranks of the Catholic Church and were filled with compassion for the father. Dad was passed over for promotion so as to relieve any unnecessary pressure on him. Bill knew the bank was lying. He noted the passover as unnecessary pressure in itself and simply got an extra job. Liz's little job joke came to pass. Dad became a warrior. He laboured at the bank five days a week and now at executive offices that needed cleaning after-hours each day. His family needed more money for the mortgage, clothing, food and whatever else nine bodies required, despite the risk of complete paternal exhaustion. He also made changes at home, deciding new shoes were held off indefinitely. All the children had school shoes with metal tips tacked on the front and back to preserve the sole as long as possible. He even tacked all thong ends – including his own. The unreported loss of a tip drew serious consequences from the hard worker who had tacked them on to prevent unnecessary wear and tear. Bill could be calm about some topics but one didn't mess around with wear and tear anymore. Bill was heard to say more than once, "This pair of shoes may even last long enough to fit young Tim one day".

Year One was a confusing time for Tim. He didn't know what shoes might mean in his future but he had enough to think about as he encountered the West social practices. The uncomfortable feelings that had penetrated the uterine wall now increased in his interactions with other household members.

Bill was in survival mode most of the time just getting paid work done. He had little time for Tim and when they were together dad's eyes never met his. Mum was awesome at feed time, the milk of the gods, but most other times she wasn't quite there with him either. The big sister was all smiles and kisses on the occasions when she did appear but she was thinking about her boyfriend 90 per cent of the time and school occupied the rest. The small sister managed maybe one unaffectionate kiss before she excused herself from the room, her face full of some unexpressed disappointment. His brothers would be spotted occasionally but their interests always lay elsewhere, except of course for Harold, who at least had the dignity to leave breastfeeding siblings alone.

Tim attempted smiling at everyone trying to make more friends. It didn't seem to work with anyone till eventually Geraldine put aside her failed sister plan and adopted a more positive approach to the babe. In contemporary language Geraldine considered Tim non-binary. Some of her former sisterhood ideas could be adapted to the youngest West. Perhaps Geraldine was another individual ahead of her time, always wanting to place flowers in Tim's hair, addressing him as 'Kim' and entertaining him/her every day with her complete collection of girly dolls.

One day Jo noticed a tip hanging off Geraldine's sandal and let her know quietly. Geraldine presented the damaged goods to dad and he trotted out the old 'Tim might get it' line. Jo was still in hearing distance. She waited till her little sister had slipped away and commented:

"Dad why do you keep saying that? Geraldine might try to fit her shoes on Tim one day but we know he isn't Cinderella. We can't encourage her in how she is treating him."

"Yes I guess I need to stop getting my genders mixed up. Sorry Jo, I'm not always thinking clearly these days."

"If she keeps it up Harold is going to have so much more ammo on Tim."

"Harold's only going through a teasing phase Jo, he will mature beyond it."

"Harold has more than one teasing phase to mature through dad."

In the second half of the year Harold's attitude to the

infant was tested. Mum asked him to carry the basinet outside in the yard while she carried out the washing basket. Tim smiled at him on the way and even Harold couldn't entirely discount the warmth of that baby smile. Harold responded out of character and drew close cheek to cheek. As it was early days for Tim, he didn't have total control over his limbs and he poked Harold's right eye. Harold took his turn to scream and after a visit to the hospital he was allowed to stay home from school for a week. With this unexpected payoff, he may even have found it in his heart to forgive his little brother. Let's hope so.

In the end Year One wasn't too bad. Tim was crawling around on all fours, exploring his surroundings and not bumping his head too often. The family was stretched in many ways but the basics of life were taken care of, much as Tim experienced inside mum. They had shelter, clothing and food most nights, certainly more than families had experienced during the war. The war was not discussed much in the West household but it provided the background to so many things that occurred within.

Both Bill and Liz had learned to persevere through the dark days of World War II. Bill had served in the artillery in Papua New Guinea while Liz had two children at home without any help from her family. Both learned a degree of independence and emotional retardation, which saw them through to the end of 1945 but it had also left wounds that lingered. They were reasonably patient parents who tried as best they could to care for all the kids but how many kids can you care for when you aren't in great shape yourself? How much had Tim been subconsciously affected by all the worries and anxieties surrounding him? These questions may not ever be answered fully for Tim, despite the fact that many psychologists consider years one to five to be the most influential years in the formation of human personality. What will become of him?

# YEAR 2 - 4.2

## *Still life, not school*

~

Tim really had enough of crawling in his second year and began walking with minor success. He had barely made his way to walking with confidence parading down the hallway showing off one of his new steps, when Liz burnt the chops one night. The kids began assembling for the evening meal, and saw smoke emerging from the kitchen. Bill inhaled and somehow the flames lit a fire in him too. He had a temper – a searing amount of temper when it finally erupted. The older kids had learned to read the signs. They made themselves scarce when the rumbling began.

"What the hell are you doing Liz?"

"Trying not to burn the chops."

"Trying isn't good enough Liz, these chops cost you know."

"I'm sorry Bill ..." her words trailed off as she began to freeze up.

"Sorry isn't good enough – why the hell do I have to do everything!" He yelled as he turned off the grill and yelled some more.

All of the older kids had already disappeared into their rooms leaving Tim to face the maelstrom alone. Tim had heard this noise before but he had never had to face it alone. He stood transfixed before his out of control father and went all numb. Tim thought, "Why is dad upset with me? I walked the whole hallway and he doesn't like it. Please stop dad. I can't handle this. Help!"

Liz scooped up Tim and ran into her bedroom – both of them crying together. Dad went on and on but eventually settled down and tried to rescue the chops. The dinner table was never a flurry of conversation amongst the Wests but that night the ensuing dinner was silent bar breathing. Someone must have enjoyed the chops a la well done.

Mud pies could also bring out the worst in dad when his youngest was about. Tim was only about two when Geraldine taught him how to make mud pies on the back verandah. She had never suffered dad's wrath about this because she had always cleaned them up before he got home. Numerous episodes of soiled verandah had led to the boys getting solid spankings from dad and their little sister was well warned.

Sadly this time Geraldine was called away to a friend's house and left Tim alone with his new skill. Mum was fully engaged inside the house and the boys were all at footy. By the time dad got home Tim looked like he had been playing footy too, covered as he was in mud from head to toe and sitting beside his proud collection of mud pies. Dad went off like a rocket and Tim thought it was just his fault again.

Doubts entered and lingered in the toddler's mind about whether or not his dad really liked him. Suspicions about mum not liking him also played with the young one's mind. The transition from breast milk to solids had been hard in the first year. Tim had to adjust to not being held very often in mum's arms. As a toddler he struggled to keep her attention when he was achieving great things such as crawling all the way across the lounge room floor or standing up for twenty seconds without holding onto anything. Mum would look at him for a moment but then look right through him to another place. She should have been awarding him an Olympic medal and singing the anthem, but no, mum just gazed away into a world that only mother knew existed.

Mum took Tim to tennis days with other mums and there he got big breasty hugs from all the ladies. Tim was still not too big to be picked up and held, so this felt great at the court but caused him to wonder why mum wasn't able to hug as good as all the other mums.

When Tim began to talk the first word was 'ball'. This was not a surprise as most of the family remembered when a backyard footy bounced off a belly. The family also noted his fascination with any object that rolled on the floor. Bill and Liz were relieved it wasn't 'dad' or 'mum' because these were words already overused in their household. Distracting the boys with all manner of balls was part of the parenting strategy to wear them out in the day so their nights were a bit free. They fully approved of Tim becoming more and more obsessed with the balls around their house. Footballs, basketballs, cricket balls, tennis balls, plastic balls and even a soccer ball were all part of the furniture inside and outside the house.

Another great distraction from reality was the increasing popularity of television. The early models were too expensive for most folks but in Tim's third year his dad was able to bring home a black and white model that became a major family focus. Balls were banned from the television room but who needed them when you had Huckleberry Hound or Bob and Dolly Dyer on the screen. Some shows held fascination for different age groups but when it first arrived at the Wests all ages were accommodated no matter what was on. It created a bond of sorts for all family members and Harold's siblings noted that his humiliation tactics began to decrease as his viewing increased. TV was quite innocent in its beginnings so it was not a primary source of incitement in Harold till years later.

Tim was able to help his mum out at times. In the days before supermarkets there were deliveries of fresh milk, vegetables and bread to your household door. He was unable to manage milk arrivals because that happened before he got out of bed, but the bread man was someone he got to know personally. Each weekday, bread would arrive about 3.00 pm and Tim had an inbuilt clock which alerted him to the impending delivery. He would hear the insertion of loaves into the bread bin and cry out "man, man" to his mum who would then open the front door and say hi to Brad. Often Brad would pick Tim up and give him a hug and mum would give Tim a hug too, so he would look forward to Brad coming every weekday. Weekends were days off for most working people so Tim could go for at least two days without a Brad or mum hug.

Weekends were sport and church time and Tim was left at home on Saturday and taken to church on Sunday but there weren't any hugs there.

As Tim developed language skills he didn't much care to speak too much anyway. He was learning to live by himself and wasn't sure whom to really trust. Mum talked even less than he did, dad was absent most of the time, and his siblings certainly couldn't be trusted. Harold had introduced him to the Hill Programme and one day mum had wondered how Tim had scratched his forearm so badly. Harold threatened him with more than mere scratches if he dobbed him in and his brothers were sworn to secrecy. Harold had compiled dossiers on them all. Tim didn't comprehend the scope of black-mail involved and thought himself abandoned by all his brothers. He thought at least one of them should have saved him from Harold's treachery.

His sisters were no better. Tim's increasing size and mobility restricted Geraldine's manipulation of him, so much so that she also became less attentive. She would soon be going to high school and her interests were increasingly outside the home, like her older sister. Jo was on the verge of leaving home entirely and Albert was soon to move into a country teaching appointment.

Backyard football had always attracted Tim's attention. When he finally gained control over his moving legs his life changed. The older boys took the game seriously playing tackle not tip. When Brendan passed the ball to three-year-old Tim as a joke for the first time, they were surprised he caught the ball and charged. They thought they would simply tolerate his involvement but Tim moved very well for someone so young. He shocked them again and again and by age four he was trying out a left foot sidestep or two. The ball obsession had taken root and it gave Tim the opportunity to express his frustrations in a fun way. "Pass the ball!" became his catchcry.

## Year 4.2 - 4.5

This time period remained a blur in Tim's mind for most of his life and it shall remain so, in you – the reader's mind, as well, until such time as his self-esteem is strong enough to withstand outside analysis.

# YEAR 4.6 – 5.5
# KINDERGARTEN

*Classtime begins*

~

Kindergarten preschools were uncommon back then. Had there been one accessible, Liz would have worked another job just to pay for Tim's attendance. He was growing up quickly and followed the pattern of hyperactivity set by his brothers. Tim was one lively lad and Liz was desperate to get him into kindergarten (also known as kindy) a year early. The cut-off date for enrolments in the following year was June 30th. Liz reckoned an extra 31 days was just a technicality because Tim was such a bright boy.

The local kindy was part of the church structure and the parish priest had to approve each child's acceptance. When Liz discovered that she began to relax. Father O'Brien was true to his Irish roots in being rather fond of his nation's whisky. It's not recorded how many bottles of Jameson were needed to gain an early entry but Tim was enrolled for the class of '63.

Despite all the issues that Tim had with his mother, next to Albert she was the most reliable human he had yet met. The primary school had no orientation programme before the commencement of term to acclimatize newcomers. It was basically getting thrown into the deep end of the pool and newcomers could sink or swim. Literal swimming lessons were still years away for Tim but they would be as problematic as this metaphorical beginning. The start day approached and mum tried to prepare him.

"Only five days to go to the start of kindy, Tim."

No answer from Tim but he thought about why she was getting rid of him.

"It's going to be lots of fun at kindy – you will make lots of friends with the other kids there."

Tim hopes the kids are more like Albert than Harold but keeps his hopes to himself. Liz has another go.

"It has a big playground where you can run as much as you like."

(This works.) "How big is the playground?"

"It's 50 times as big as our backyard and you can play cricket and touch footy."

"No tackle?"

"No it's a hard surface. You can play handball and cricket and chasings without tripping over holes or rocks. Lots of fun."

"So we can play all day?"

"No you play in the breaks between classes. You sit down and listen to the teacher inside your classroom. She will ask you to colour in or draw some things. Afterwards you go outside and play."

Tim went quiet again as he considered these propositions. He liked to draw but he liked to play footy more and he wondered what things he wasn't being told about. He grabbed a footy and went outside to play.

K-Day came one Tuesday morning. It didn't start well because dad had taken up residence in the outside toilet as he did each morning. He always spent at least 20 minutes there reading the Sydney Morning Herald without interruption. This applied significant pressure on the inside toilet as the other eight individuals vied for position. Tim was normally able to go before everyone else, and he did so, but nerves brought on an unexpected second wave and he wet his undies in the queue. Mum got a new pair and with hours of freedom so close, she controlled her own temper and Tim barely noticed the flash in her eyes. The uncertainty of the day weighed on Tim and he realized how much mum did for him. He looked at her as she kissed dad goodbye and thought she was the most beautiful woman in the world. This didn't help at the time because if she was the most beautiful, then the teacher could only be a step down in the wrong direction.

Mum held his little hand as they crossed the road to wait for the school bus. It stopped outside their house.

The bus driver smiled at Tim as he placed his foot onto the first step but Tim wouldn't let go of mum's hand. Liz didn't want to frighten her son more than he already was so she didn't shake him off her finger. He had a very tight hold but Liz said to the bus driver, "I don't have a bus pass Ben, but my big Tim has one."

The bus driver explained to Tim, "Only big boys have their own bus pass Tim and today is your day. Your sister used to catch this bus and now it's your turn."

He released his grip without being entirely convinced and mum smiled and waved frantically as the bus drove away and then turned up the hill. Tim's heart now beat as frantically as mum's hands had waved goodbye. He remained tense during the whole bus ride and the day as it unfolded. He met his teacher at the end of the ride and she looked OK but she only had time for a quick greeting before she welcomed another kindy kid.

It was all very bewildering for Tim. Some of the kids already knew each other and they played together while others like Tim stood at a distance and tried to work out what was happening. A bell rang and the older kids began to walk slowly to form patterns that once again increased the bewilderment factor for the newbies. The kindy teacher approached her recruits and led them into a line-up that resembled the other classes. Some of the older kids made faces at Tim and his companions when their teacher wasn't looking. This didn't improve the odds of these school children being like Tim's favourite brother Albert.

The school principal was an old nun who had already issued a long list of orders the day before to the older classes who needed to look after the kindergarten children. Hence the newcomers weren't subjected to a half an hour standing in the summer heat like classes one to four had endured 24 hours earlier. But would the older kids embrace their new responsibilities wholeheartedly or would they behave like most older children in positions of power?

Kindy was dismissed after five minutes of the principal trying to muster up a smile and then walked to their classroom. Teacher allocated their seats in alphabetical order, starting with the letter 'A'. Tim wondered if there were going to be enough seats left by the time his name was called. This was not because he knew the alphabet yet, (scheduled for second term), rather he always felt he was last all the time. The name West was a long way back in the order of things and this would fit in with his developing world view. His apprehension was almost fulfilled as the number of kids left standing was reduced to two. He looked at the only other kid next to him but then he heard his name called out. He claimed the last seat available. Unfortunately the kid with the surname starting with 'Z' had to wait another ten minutes for the teacher to scramble up another desk and chair for him. In the meantime all the class was exhorted to remain seated quietly. This 'sit quietly' thing became a constant rule. It didn't make sense to Tim but he guessed it wouldn't be like that forever.

The morning passed pretty quickly listening to Mrs Connor and colouring in lots of pictures. Morning tea was time to test how big the playground really was. Tim ran and ran. By lunchtime he was running around again, too busy to make new friends. He gorged himself at the water bubblers just before it was time to go back into class but he felt fine having done half a dozen laps of the playground.

Mrs Connor started reading a book to the class and some of the kids began to fall asleep. Everything was so quiet except for the teacher's voice and Tim had to go to the toilet. He had used the toilet at morning tea but forgot to during lunch. It was becoming more urgent as he sat quietly listening to the story and getting more and more anxious. Tim asked himself, *"Do I interrupt and ask to go to the toilet or not?"* His thoughts became more and more confused and then he could hold on no more. He was at the back of the class but a pool of wee began to make its way toward the front of the class. Tim started crying and Mrs Connor went into action. It wasn't the first time this had happened and Tim was helped out of the class by the principal without too much fanfare. Some kids didn't even see what had happened but it was the end of the day for Tim.

A 4th Class girl was assigned to take Tim home to the front door of his house. He was handed over to his mum who got him in the bath and soon he was asleep on top of his bed ... all problems solved. It wasn't the greatest introduction to St Mary's but it wasn't brought up again in the West household or even at school (where there were probably a few kids who, at the very least, dampened their undies that first day). It did however become one of Tim's clearest early memories. He felt he failed somehow.

The kid with the 'Z' surname became Tim's best friend. Sam Zammit was his full name – at least his full Australian name – the Maltese original must have been longer. In those days most caucasian locals knew Maltese immigrants as 'wogs' but such bigotry did not exist in the West household. Dad knew the war was won by many nationalities and he didn't allow the cultural norm to affect his respect for most tribes and tongues. Tim was unaware of such influences but he and Sam were made for each other on that first day when they searched each other eyes just before the last desk was assigned. The next day they ran around the playground perimeter together and Sam didn't get tired like the other kids. 'Maltese endurance' his dad called it and both boys needed some endurance because other class members shunned them.

Sam would visit the Wests especially when Tim was able to talk mum into allowing train tracks to be set up the full length of the hall. Even Geraldine and Bob would be interested in helping them set up and it was fun trying to build a track that didn't allow the windup engine to fly off in the middle of the final curve. The team of four recognised it was best policy to plan these days when Harold was out of the house at a friend's place. Liz thought it was nice to see Bob talking openly to his siblings as the engine whizzed around the countryside,

"Hey Ged, do you remember when the engine went off the track and Brendan caught it before it went straight into Tim's head?"

Geraldine replied, "Of course I do, it was a catch and a half."

"Without that catch Tim", said Bob, "you'd probably still have a cracked skull. The engine came off at the end of the long straight and you were crawling right there."

Geraldine added, "Yes and it was lucky that Brendan was there too, not Harold." (At the mention of Harold's name the conversation sort of closed down as they noticed mum's lifted eyebrow.)

Tim got used to going to school like most kids. Playtime was always the best time with Sam at his side. However the real good thing about school is that terms do end. Holidays take place four times a year and the summer break in Australia goes for six beautiful weeks. By the time Tim was at school Bill and Liz were able to afford to go away for a camping holiday at the beach. Hence Tim was introduced to the NSW Central Coast and its abundance of water and waves. Toukley, The Entrance and then Avoca Beach became annual pilgrimages that fed the spirit of the entire family.

Jo and Albert stayed home and just visited the site

for a day or two as their lives outgrew the family circle. Albert had a Mini Minor. The new family Kombi van could almost accommodate seven individuals with gear comfortably – somehow they all squeezed in. Tim loved it when Albert came to visit because he would take him out into the big waves and help him stay out of the rips. Rips could reputedly take you as far as New Zealand and with Tim not having had any swimming lessons yet he might not make it.

# 1ST TO 3RD CLASS

*Nuntime education*

~

The inevitability of school restarting had not yet imprinted itself upon Tim and the summer holidays seemed like they would never end. During the holidays a family moved in next door with two brothers – one being a year older and the other a year younger than Tim. This was perfect because Tim became good friends with them both. When the brothers fell out Tim became the negotiator. If he failed to settle the argument, he still had one to play with. However when it came time to go back to school, Tim became conflicted in his mind.

His neighbours went to the public school up the other hill, not St Mary's. Meeting people who weren't Catholic was new for Tim. He had assumed they were Catholics who didn't attend church very often. Without any real understanding of religious systems outside his family's realm, Tim concluded they were Publics not Catholics. The Smiths in fact didn't go to church every

Sunday. They were quite irreligious in comparison to the Wests' hectic schedule, which cluttered up their lives week in week out. St Mary's shaped so much of Tim's life. He had religion class everyday, compulsory Sunday attendance and regular praying of the rosary at home. By the time Tim made it to 4th Class he realized that his neighbours weren't Publics but Protestants and years later even more specifically Church of Englanders. The families had become friends despite having religious differences. Unlike many Aussies Bill had broad spiritual views. They had enabled him to convert to his spouse's brand of faith without much fuss. His expansive style of understanding religion was inherited by most of his kids and further expanded beyond the current limits by some.

The standout events of 1st Class for Tim were neither academic nor religious. The car races around the square had a special place in his heart. He wasn't issued an early car licence, he just had a vivid imagination along with the other 1st Classers. Each day you could choose what car you were for the day and you would race around the marked playground square. The number of laps varied so some were sprints – others long distance. Two laps comprised the shortest race and this was hardest because all four corners were sharp. Cars had to slow down so as to not spin out and lose their place to the 10 or so competitors close on the bumper bar. Choice of car tended to rely on what dad owned or admired. Ford and Holden dominated but some kids went for the Bathurst winner of 1963 – a Cooper S. Tim saw the winning car on TV and thought it was the same as his brother's Mini Minor. A Mini was always his first choice. Tim was fast and he won a lot of heats but a Holden always beat him in the final. The driver was Rod Redford.

His teacher that year wasn't one of the nuns who prowled the playground always looking out for lawbreakers. Miss Ryan was a friendly woman who cared for the kids and helped them to focus on the work they had to complete for the syllabus. Like his Kindergarten teacher she never used the cane on any of the students and these women reminded Tim of mum on her best days. Both of these teachers weren't given to having tantrums or sitting in a chair, sulking most of the day.

Tim eased into the second scholastic year enjoying subjects like Reading and Projects. He began to make friends with a lot more kids, mainly racers. He even had a secret crush on a girl who kept smiling at him in the playground. Neither of them had the courage or motivation to move across the boy/girl demarcation line. Boys raced and girls skipped and never the twain shall meet in post-war Australia.

It was in 2$^{nd}$ Class that Roman Catholic religious education really took off. Not only did Tim get a dedicated-to-God nun for a teacher, it was also the year that kids were to take their First Communion. Yes, these seven-year-olds are coming of age in terms of their participation in church services this year. Sunday was always mysterious and nearly always boring for Tim. Participants stood up and sat down and stood up again, sang and then knelt down and stood up, got fed up and so on. The priest mainly spoke in Latin but even English would have been incomprehensible to the younger attendees.

The interesting time was when people older than seven went up to the front of the church and got something to eat. Tim was told it helps everyone to become good like Jesus. The teaching nun didn't seem any better for taking communion, as she prowled the playground, catching and caning kids. She also described the ritual as a special time of remembering Jesus. This only added to Tim's confusion because he picked up early on that Jesus died a long time ago. How then could he meet Jesus? You can't remember someone you haven't met. Despite all the confusion about his teacher and her teaching, Tim saw on Sunday that all the adults in the congregation participated in the communion ceremony. He figured it's just a part of growing up and maybe he can work it out later.

Getting dressed up in your best clothes was part of every Sunday but Tim wasn't ready for the spectacle that was about to take place on this special Sunday. He wasn't keen about getting more dressed up than usual for the service but when he saw mum in her new dress and hat bought especially for today, he felt better about it. He had to wear a tie and his new best clothes.

"Come on Tim get dressed in the clothes I've laid out for you on the bed."

"It really is a special day mum, you are so dressed up."

"Of course it's special today Tim. You get to share in Holy Communion for the first time. You and all your classmates will receive it from the bishop and then all of us will follow. The whole family gets to share Communion today."

Dad intervenes, "If you don't start getting dressed Tim you might be the last one getting it today."

Mum protests, "Leave him alone Bill, we still have lots of time. Today belongs to Tim."

"Can you help me with the tie mum, I'm still not very good at doing it up?"

"Yes we want you to look your best today."

"Just don't lose track of the time Liz, we have to be there early so they have time to get the kids organised properly."

"Oh Bill, we won't be late today and I will make sure your youngest is ready on time."

When they arrived at the school for the final preparation, Tim was shocked to see all the girls dressed up in white frills and swirls that reminded him of angels and fairies. The dress code for Roman Catholic First Communion is right up there with weddings and funerals. It is a tradition held in high regard. Not only is the dress code at its zenith, the segregation of males and females is totally dismissed for the day.

Tim was assigned one of the girls whom he was to accompany across the road and into the front row of the church. She was the one who looked at him in the playground. Her name was Cathy. They smiled at each other as their hands were placed together. Heart rates went up. They continued to hold hands as they walked and it felt good for Tim. Words only came to the edge of Tim's lips after the service commenced. He would possibly have talked to her during the service had not all adult eyes been on the new communicants. His mother and other ladies were wiping tears from their eyes, while the men stared intently at their sons.

The boy/girl demarcation line was totally disregarded today. Some kids even thought that maybe they would fall in love with their partner before the end of the day. Some might have but the next day at school the demarcation line would be reinstated. Cathy and Tim would remain on their allotted sides and Tim would conclude that girls were very sweet but too hard to talk to.

During the service the intermingling of the sexes attired in all their respective glory made an impressive sight in St Mary's. The bishop was especially proud of the boys and girls arrayed before him. He prattled on for quite a while about some of the children taking up holy vocations in the future, though what this was still eluded most of the young participants.

When the fateful moment approached to receive the body of Jesus, Tim was caught by surprise at how hard the biscuit was and he found it difficult to swallow. He did not feel any better for his participation and the mystery of this Jesus religion continued to be just that – highly mysterious. Of course he kept his opinion to himself as all the kids were congratulated on their spectacular start. Parents hugged and kissed them and said how beautiful it all was and Tim could only agree. There was however a bonus for Tim when they got home. On the dining table there sat a communion cake that Aunty Helen had cooked especially for this day. Tim scored the biggest piece and thought that this religious stuff isn't all bad after all.

When the kids arrived in class the next day, the nun's attitude to them remained unaffected by their being welcome at the communion table. The bishop said how God loved all these children but it seemed the nun wasn't listening yesterday because there wasn't any love coming out of her mouth toward them today.

Sister Agnes was on playground duty, "Briggs what are you doing next to the girls' toilet?"

"I was just getting a tennis ball back."

"What is the rule about the toilets and who can enter?"

"Only girls can cross the yellow line."

"Are you a girl Briggs?"

"I was only there a second."

"You should have waited for one of the girls to get it for you."

"There weren't any girls around."

"Silence! Come over here. Next time you wait. A girl will come if you wait. This is going to help your memory

Briggs." He got two cuts of the cane right there in front of the whole playground. She announced to the onlookers, "Follow the rules or it will be you next time." The kids had never seen a playground caning before, offenders were normally whisked off inside a building. Sister Agnes was one hard lady and Tim hoped that Jesus would give her some love because she didn't seem to have much at her disposal. She expected everyone to do exactly as she said or else.

Tim learned to be a good student. Sister Agnes only wanted good work done in her class. Lazy work or bad work or even worse, work that wasn't done was always punishable. Thankfully the cane was not always the chosen instrument. The dunce hat, the bad chair at the back of the classroom, and notes to parents were other punishments that ensured kids that could work – would work. Tim was quite bright and he excelled in all his subjects. He even came first place overall in some terms and his parents got used to seeing high performance report cards. One hundred out of one hundred occurred more than once in multiple subjects. Maintaining the high standard was expected and Tim himself could be disappointed if he didn't get full marks for his favourite subjects.

His above average achievements continued into 3rd Class. Tim was good at academic stuff like arithmetic and reading as well as creative areas like art and music. He was especially good at writing and drawing and his teacher encouraged him to illustrate the stories he would write. His teacher was not a nun and Tim appreciated how she liked good work but didn't insist on it like Sister Agnes. He became more outspoken in class this year and he felt free to express himself more often than ever before.

Miss Trimble began teaching the class Australian history and how Captain James Cook discovered Australia (Revisionist history was scarce back then). Tim was fascinated by the tales of how the Endeavour sailed up the east coast of Australia mapping the coastline as they went. Miss gave them an assignment to complete by the end of the following week. Tim set about doing his very best to illustrate the major role the Endeavour played in the odyssey up the coast and the delay on the reef that was almost a complete shipwreck. Tim very carefully drew a picture of Cook's vessel to illustrate his story. He took a long time to draw the outlines and then carefully colour them all in. It was his best drawing to date.

The day came to hand in the assignment and present it to the class. Tim briefly explained his story and showed his pictures along with it. Miss was really impressed and most of the kids gasped when they saw how beautiful the drawing was of the Endeavour. Tim was feeling super proud and he was given a five star mark for his excellent work. However this was not the end of the story. In the next break his classmates came up to him and started accusing, "You didn't draw that picture."

"Yes I did," replied Tim quickly.

"No you didn't. You aren't big enough to draw that good," said another.

"How do you know I'm not?"

"I know you aren't big enough," added the class bully.

"Your dad must have done it," suggested the bully's sidekick.

"No I did it!" yelled Tim

"Your brother did it!" came the sidekick's second thought.

"You're lying West," piped up yet another.

"You're a liar, liar, liar!" cried out the original accuser.

"No I'm not, not, not!" cried back Tim.

"Liar, liar, liar," became the refrain as Agnes noticed what was happening and everyone shut up and walked away. Tim ran.

The hard thing for Tim was that so many kids were saying this. Maybe a dozen kids accused him of being a liar because he wasn't old enough to draw a picture that good. His brother or dad must have drawn it. What had been a triumph turned into a tragedy. Tim kept telling them he had drawn it but none of the kids believed him. He had been on the verge of breaking down in tears but held it in.

When he broke away from the abusers, he was able to run some of his anger off around the playground. He was also in the habit of running home after the finish of school and this day he was especially fast. Most days he raced the Barley brothers home and he won easily that day.

When he finally got into the privacy of his own room, he broke down and cried a river and couldn't believe how cruel and stupid his classmates were. This would not be the only day in Tim's schooling that involved false accusations by multiple ignoramuses. Tim decided to keep his best drawings private from that day on and it wasn't until he changed schools that his artistic abilities would be under public scrutiny again.

His final year at St Mary's was also the year that Tim entered the world of organised rugby union. It was a rugby ball that ushered him into the world and it was the game of rugby that ushered its way into Tim's heart for the next 20 years. St Mary's decided to start a team in the Under 8 Eastwood District Rugby Competition. Rod Redford would become the star player of the team but it was Tim who would make a name in the adult arena years later.

The first year of rugby was a year of learning the basics. The players were too young to understand much other than "Get that ball and run!" And hopefully it was in the right direction. From the sideline the game looked a lot like a perpetual roving pack of sheep. Kids clustered around the ball wildly throwing arms and legs at it in attempts to get it into the hands of their fastest player. Occasionally fast boy Rod did get the ball on the fringes of the chaos and he would run around the opposing team to score. He was the sole back in the team, everyone else were forwards foraging for that elusive golden fleece. Tim foraged harder than anyone else and halfway through the season he found himself on the fringes of the mayhem and someone passed the ball to him. He took off from his own 25-yard line and there was no one in front of him. So much space was a rare thing and as he ran on freely, he accelerated. He could hear breathing behind him as he slowed near the try line but a desperate lunge only removed his collar, it didn't stop his first try. Tim replayed the try over and over in his head for weeks and the glow of glory he felt at the time never faded away completely. A 75-yard try was something even Rod had yet to achieve and his confidence grew more and more on the footy field.

St Mary's made the grand final in their first season. Both teams had a real chance of winning as they both had a number one star player. The opposition star didn't get injured in the game. Sadly Rod only lasted half a game. The opposition's big guy smashed St Mary's star just after half time and their star took over. They won by 20 points. Tim scored a try in the second half but the pain of losing that final lingered and made him more determined to come out a winner next year. The pennant he was awarded for being a grand finalist was good but not good enough. He told Sam, "Next year is going to be our year".

Tim would move to the preparatory school located at the high school his brothers attended. He was moving up in the world like his older brothers. He knew the colour of the jersey would be different, the same tricolour one Bob wore to footy. What Tim didn't know yet was that next year he would be playing in a different team and a different code. Football had mitigated his setbacks at St Mary's and he had begun to feel that maybe he belonged at school. He hadn't yet met the big school's principal.

# 4ᵀᴴ CLASS

## *Marist education begins*

~

Every boy applying for entry at Marist Brothers Ryde attended a compulsory meeting with the principal. Each boy had a paternal escort, unless of course dad was absent, then it was mum on guard. Mr West and Tim drove in silence to the school one afternoon during the school holidays. In Tim's mind this in itself seemed a massive infringement on children's holiday rights, let alone what was to come.

It was not an easy visit. The principal was a large individual with eyes that glistened sharply, showing something that could be called malice. Brother Brendan was his name and he laid down the law about weekend sport as well as weekday activities. Marist Brothers Ryde was a proud participant in the Marist Brothers Rugby League competitions. League was clearly a superior game said those malevolent eyes and all boys exhibiting talent were required to play rugby league on Thursday and Saturday for the school. Brendan had heard about the 75-yard try and Tim was forced against his will to play league with Rod on Thursday and Saturday. Thursday was fine because it replaced class time but Sam didn't make the cut and would only play with the rest of the underachievers in the Saturday Rugby Union competition.

When they got to the car after the meeting Tim cried out, "It's not fair!"

Bill tried to lower the level of anxiety in the vehicle, "Yes it's hard Tim. Brother Brendan wants to win the competition this year and he knows you can help do that."

"But I want to play with Sam and my other friends."

"Sam isn't as good a player as you and Rod and you really wanted to win the grand final last year. This year with better players you can win a grand final."

"I want to win with Sam in the team."

"You can play with Sam in the backyard and at his place and at the oval after school. You can still see lots of Sam."

Tim wasn't convinced but pushing too hard brought out The Voice, which only had one paternal volume … loud! He could never beat dad in an argument, so he just shut up. Bill thought he had done a good job but Tim was cut to the heart and he cried freely when he got home to his bedroom. Bill was outside somewhere and didn't hear any crying.

When school started Tim was excited to be wearing the uniform his brothers had worn, another sign of growing up in the world. He was leaving the small schoolyard of St Mary's for the wide open spaces of high school. It was still all concrete but there were three large playgrounds, two with cricket nets and one with a basketball court. The footy oval was outside school grounds down the hill a bit but accessed during physical exercise (PE classes). The glorious freedom of the holidays was over but there were upsides to Marist Brothers. Brother Alexander was his class teacher and he was sympathetic, helping his students adapt to a new environment.

Tim got on with the boy who sat next to him at the desk they shared. Adrian was a tall one but friendly with everyone – not just the big boys. Playing cricket in the morning at the nets was heaps of fun even though it wasn't his game. Handball and brandings were highlights and helped Tim make new friends. The first couple of months were a honeymoon.

It was as Tim got to know other teachers, reminding him of the principal, that suspicions about this school increased. There was one brother in particular, a fit, wiry athletic type who expected everyone else, regardless of shape or size, to share his athletic abilities. He revealed a glimpse of his true nature one day at assembly. It was not a revelation of love.

Brother Decimus was in control of the playground this day. He could espy the entire play area from atop a rock wall that separated the brothers' residence from the school grounds. The boys were all playing cricket or brandings. Adrian was normally an active participant in the ball games before the whistle blew for assembly but not this morning. Students were told to stand up straight for inspection and everyone obeyed or else you got a clip behind the ears. Adrian was committing the sin of not standing up straight. Brother Decimus spotted him. The ear clipper was prowling around sinners on the other side, so when Adrian didn't respond to the first or second Decimus command to stand up straight, he was ordered loudly, "Come to the front McConaughy!"

Decimus berated the boy as he slowly approached, his face a cold sneer of contempt. When Adrian finally arrived at the front he promptly fainted. He fell face first into the wall upon which Decimus stood. Blood flowed and his front teeth would require surgery. There was no sign of empathy on Decimus' face for the fallen eight-year-old. Other brothers rushed to the rescue. Even the clipper expressed concern for Adrian. Throughout the entire incident the playground commander maintained his sneer. Decimus was the under 10 football coach. Tim and Adrian were under nine, clearly a reprieve for both of them this year. There was no reprieve for Adrian from these injuries now though. He was absent from school for five weeks.

Tim was up the back of the class missing his new friend. His desk was in the corner and the middle desk next to him was empty all the time, perhaps to undermine any revolutionary fervour that could emerge from the back row. He developed another degree of independence as he laboured alone in the last row. He felt freer up the back of the class and he could see most of the tricks boys got up to as they got bored. Tim had inside information on offenders but it never occurred to him to use it like Harold.

Brother Alexander was the under nine coach and he treated his players with respect for their tender age. There wasn't any tenderness in the players when they were on the field but after the game the boys may need soft words. Last year's grand final hung over at least two of his charges. With the finals only a few weeks away they lost a game they had been confident of winning. The team was used to winning, so when they lost a game it was like the end of the world for some. It was a timely reminder to never underestimate a determined opponent and Alexander noted this. He was able to console them without pampering to them, instructing them to remain focused on playing hard all the time, not just when you feel like it. Back in the classroom the same principle applied. Alexander didn't get angry often but he did expect all assigned work to be finished on time or else. Tim and Four Red learned to work and play hard consistently.

After school Tim and Sam would discuss all the important aspects of how to win handball games or avoid being hit with the brandings ball. The game of brandings didn't involve a red-hot iron, though Decimus may have entertained the idea in his fantasy life. Brandings is a ball game where one child has to throw an old tennis ball accurately and hit another. The brandee then becomes part of the branding team until everyone is branded except the last boy who is the winner. Both Tim and Sam were pretty good at avoiding being branded until the end of most games. Sam needed to be good because he was a dark target among a lotta white boys. Handball was a much safer recreation. It simply involved using your hand to slap a ball past your opponent's hand. Winter approached and with it increasing cold. Sam suggested an innovation in handball.

"Hey Tim, do you think I could wear a glove when it gets really cold?"

"Wear a glove in handball? No way that's a sissy thing to do."

"But you know what it's like on a cold morning, the fast hits hurt heaps."

"You just have to take it."

"Well what if you already have a sore hand?"

"Sore hand, no play. Come on Sam you're already a bulls eye in brandings, if you wear a glove in handball, you won't be able to play brandings."

"What do you mean, I can't play?"

"I mean you won't want to play. You're already a target, wear a glove and your bulls eye gets bigger."

"But I'm one of the best at not being hit."

"Yes you are and so am I but you can bet we'll both be getting hit more if you start wearing a glove."

"Maybe you're right – it's just an idea. My hand is sore."

"All of you is gonna be sore if they hit you up close mate."

Any up close brand from someone who didn't like you, was one of the most painful hits you could receive at Marist Brothers. Handball was less physically demanding so Sam backed off. It was still a fiercely competitive sport in the playground and Sam had reason to be concerned about a sore hand. Some boys with good hands could be close to tears if they stayed on a losing streak. Tears were reserved for serious injuries; girls cry/boys don't.

One measure of manhood was in how well you endured cuts of the cane. Six of the best may bring a touch of moisture to even a seasoned offender's eye but only at the second to last cut. The first four hardly hurt at all according to an unspoken school tradition. If that rule was broken the after school bullies would find out and find you.

Tim learned to be a good boy. He avoided getting the cane in his first year at Marist Brothers. Alexander never had cause to use corporal punishment on Tim … that was reserved for the years ahead and it was something that would remain with Tim beyond his years of schooling.

Back at home base mum and dad rarely encouraged their youngest. Good marks had become the expectation in his report cards, distinctions taken for granted as a baseline. Of course complete perfection was not expected at home and school because only Jesus is perfect but standards close to perfect were. If high marks were not maintained subtle suggestions of parental disgust emerged and shamed a sensitive son into working harder next time. Even football became a problem when mum and dad came to the games because dad expected his talented son to win and win well – all the time. Tim won the grand final with his new team but it didn't feel as good without Sam being at his side. When he received the champion pennant it felt the same as the runners-up pennant he received last year. Rod received the best and fairest award, Tim the most improved.

On the way home Liz spoke up, "Congratulations Tim, you played so well today and you won the most improved award."

"Thanks mum. I wish Sam was here." Sam's comp went longer than Tim's so he was playing his last round somewhere else.

Bill interrupted, "You won today Tim. You are the premiers, you should be happy."

"Yeah it was a good game and Rod didn't get injured."

"And next year you might be able to win best and fairest too," said Bill.

"Is Rod moving away?"

"No I just mean that you are getting better." (Perhaps an encouragement from Bill.)

"Yeah."

"I hear your coach next year will make sure you become premiers again."

"Yeah maybe."

"When we get home you can put up your pennant next to last year's and stand proud Tim."

"Yeah dad."

Home was more habitable when Albert returned during school holidays. In winter he drove Tim to the oval to practice and in summer they would drive the hour together to the beach. Albert would listen to Tim as he talked about dad's temper and mum's moods and Tim always felt better afterwards.

One autumn Albert took Sam and Tim to the Blue Mountains to see the Three Sisters at Echo Point. Tim had been there with his parents before, so he took pride in being able to tell Sam all he knew about the mountains. Albert was impressed how much he knew especially about the Leura Cascades and the Federal Pass Walk, which went down into the valley below the Sisters. Tim loved walking in the bush in the cool of the day, smelling the eucalyptus and discovering coves filled with ferns and waterfalls.

Albert knew things were hard for Tim at home. Mum was always moody these days and dad was there in body but not much in spirit. Dad did not appreciate being woken in the middle of the night. Bedwetting days were over for Tim but he now suffered from an occasional asthma attack in the middle of the night. He would struggle for breath and try to wake up mum but dad usually roused first, grumpy as hell. It usually went something like this:

"What are you doing Tim?"

Tim responds as much as he is able, "Da....."

"Speak up boy!"

"I ca … br …"

"Oh no, asthma again."

Tim nods.

"You put the kettle on, I'll get some eucalyptus."

Tim hastens to the kitchen and Bill gets up mumbling, "Why does this always happen at 3.00am? A working man needs his sleep, bloody hell."

Tim pretends not to hear. The kettle boils and Bill gets the mixture right and hands the tea towel to Tim. "You'll be right now Tim … I'm off to bed."

Tim thinks, "I need to start breathing again dad, bed can wait." He breathes in the eucalyptus fumes. As he inhales more of the sweet steam his normal breathing slowly returns. Soon he will be able to sleep again.

As far as he could work out from events like this, Tim was an inconvenience to this family. Ged hardly spoke to him these days. Bob and Brendan spent a lot of time at friends' places. Harold was still at home, still teasing any available sibling, especially the youngest. Harold nicknamed Tim 'Louie the Fly'. Louie was famous in Mortein World for spreading disease with the greatest of ease. It was a metaphor that Tim protested hard against but Harold wasn't someone who listened to complaining brothers, especially now he was the eldest sibling in the West household. Who needs schoolyard bullies when you have a home-grown version custom built into the family home?

Albert would try to get Tim to think outside the home. He told Tim about his pupils' antics in the classroom. Peashooters firing from one side of the room to the other were not often easy to identify. Tim had seen some Four Red radicals have a go at this recreational activity but all were caught and caned as far as he had seen. Albert's students were older and more experienced so their assaults had better timing. Albert rarely saw the actual crime itself, so he had to learn to read the faces of the guilty parties. He often got more than one confession just from body language. Some boys couldn't hide their glee. Albert didn't use the cane – he loved the kids he taught. Tim wished he was still the eldest at home and even a teacher at his school. Next year Decimus would be his football coach and class teacher. Peashooting in the classroom would probably be postponed till the following year when the chances of discovery would be less than a hundred percent.

# 5<sup>TH</sup> CLASS

*This is education?*

~

Tim had summed up his 5th Class teacher over the holidays with some ancient insight, "He will probably be a tyrant king like Agamemnon."

Sam asked, "Who is that?"

"The guy who kept the Trojan War going, not caring how many men he lost."

"Shit I hope you're wrong about that."

"Yep, old King Agi lost his brother and thousands more and he kept driving them on. Decimus didn't care about Adrian when he fell and I doubt he will care about us."

Tim had heard about the Trojan War and he thought the Greek leader who lusted after war and power wore boots that Decimus could well fit into. This contemporary tyrant didn't shoot arrows at his pupils but rather fast, well-directed pieces of chalk that could also draw blood. He was not known as a patient man but he was a thorough researcher. Decimus knew the academic history of all his underlings and knew it was his job to improve these children, expecting each class member to improve in all subjects. He may have thought 120 out of 100 was too much to demand from those who got perfect scores last year but 110 could work. He wanted all his boys to strive in that spirit of overachievement. If the boys did better than they did last year then he looked better too.

The boys had already been introduced to a competitive spirit by the hierarchical system that characterized all the years at Marist Brothers Ryde. Boys were graded into three different colours: the red class, the green class and the blue class. High achievers, average achievers and below average nobodies is how it worked. Each year you could go up a division or down depending on your results. Marist boys needed no education about the way sporting teams were promoted and relegated from first and second divisions because so many had personally experienced a change of colour in the new year. Decimus knew all the colours past and present of each of his boys. Being in his red class meant that no one would drop to green next year because he will drive them all to the limits of their academic powers. Tim was in red last year and scored a couple of 100s out of a 100. He would have to work extra hard to avoid salvos of weaponised chalk coming his way or worse.

Brother Decimus spent much of the first day in lecture mode. "You are men now and you are red class men. You will uphold the reputation of this school by your hard work in class this year. Some of you will do the same by your hard work on the sporting field this year. Determination and strength are yours to command and you will command them. The green and blue boys are not as good as you. You are the best of the best and you will improve your marks this year."

On and on he went and Tim wondered if Agamemnon gave speeches this long to Achilles and co. When the monologue finally concluded, Decimus asked if there were any questions. Despite the length of the listening time no one had fallen asleep. One boy at the front had nodded his head early on and felt a clip on the ear so fast that everyone focused full attention from that point on. Strangely Tim found a question on his lips, "Sir, isn't footy meant to be fun not hard work?"

"It might be fun for some but it's hard work that wins grand finals."

"But we won our grand final last year and it was fun."

"Don't contradict me boy. Brother Alexander got lucky last year and this year it won't be luck that gets the trophy, it will be hard work. No more questions."

Tim would not challenge his teacher again, at least not outside his own head. He focused on working hard to become an inconspicuous member of Five Red. He got a seat as far away from the front of the class as possible. It was one of the few advantages of having your surname start with 'W'.

Friday was the best school day before 1968 because the weekend was only hours away. Decimus spoiled it by holding exhausting tests every Friday: spelling, comprehension, arithmetic, social studies, science, religion and even writing were comprehensively examined at week's end. Why did he test religion on Friday when we had religion tests every other day? The catechism of the Roman Catholic Church always had a daily question and answer. Toward the end of the lesson Decimus had the boys memorise the answer and then randomly test a few boys. He would then throw in a couple of questions from previous lessons like "Aiken, what is a mortal sin?"

Aiken's eyes widen, brain gears go into action, "A sin that can only be forgiven ... in confession ... to a priest, Sir."

"Isn't there another way it can be forgiven Aiken?"

"Umm ... that's right ... aaah perfect act of contrition can do it."

"Correct Aiken, all of you will need to employ at least one of these ways to make it to heaven. Can anyone tell me a particular mortal sin?"

Silence descends on the room. No volunteers present themselves.

"Barnes! Name a mortal sin." Barnes' face clouds over as he considers the delivery of the question itself could be a mortal sin. He recovers, "... not going to church on Sunday Sir."

"Bit slow but correct. Rossi! Name another."

"Umm … adultery … Sir."

"Correct Rossi! I think we need to leave it there for now. Boys you need to keep going to church on Sunday or you will be in trouble."

Tim thought, *"Just being in your class means I'm in trouble"*.

Failure at any of the above could mean punishment of some kind. Extra homework, tongue thrashing in front of everyone, sometimes with spittle thrown in, dunce chair at class front, a walk to the principal's office, a note to the parents – these were all part of an underachiever's life.

The cane wasn't normally used for test results but failing to complete homework meant two cuts of the cane, one for each hand. Use of the cane needed to be evenly distributed to each hand in turn, so as to prevent serious injury. Apparently not all the teachers at Ryde followed this rule. Tales of a boy getting six of the best on his left hand circulated. The rumours said that teacher didn't realize that he was actually left-handed. He had wanted to make a point to this repeat offender and the boy's parents got the point and moved him to another school. No one knew who the teacher was because it had taken place behind closed doors during break time when three teachers had whisked the bully away. Three names were known, one offender for certain in their midst but no certainties. Absolute truth was reserved for the religious realm at Ryde. Fighting was against the rules and it was a good rule. It lined up with the fifth commandment to not kill and most of the students at Ryde agreed it was good.

The problem with Decimus is that he made up rules that only made sense to him. When his rules extended to footy they only further perplexed Tim and his team-mates. Training time was doubled from 45 minutes to 90 minutes as the minimum, and training always started with four laps of the oval. If you were late it was five laps – that was the rule. This is the under 10s not the under 18s but apparently the boys were men now and their coach treated them as such. Any talkback was met with another lap of the oval. Coach would instruct his players, "You must complete four out of four tackles every time our team has the ball." (Back then it was a four tackle rule not six.) "You must protect the ball at all times, no long passes. Don't drop the ball." Some players would protest, "But Sir, I can pass the ball a long way and it works sometimes."

"Taking unnecessary chances is what lost you games last year. This year we aren't going to lose a game. You are going to be the fittest, most well drilled outfit on the park and you will win."

"But I want to pass it long if I see our winger in the clear," declares the halfback.

"Are you listening to me? It might look good when it works but it doesn't always work, so don't do it."

The players don't answer but they all think, "But that's no fun!" Tim of course didn't say anything because he had learnt his lesson about questioning the Decimator earlier in the year.

Anyway Saturday did eventually arrive despite the academic roadblocks and overlong training sessions. This was the day that Tim tried to hold onto fun. Footy games still had a fun component because during the game coach was confined to one side of the field and you couldn't hear him from the other side. Neither men nor boys are machines, sometimes they throw a sensational long pass and the recipient scores a try despite it being in breach of a coach's instructions. Tim had a good pass as well as sneaky sidesteps so he was one of the improvisers who were often berated rather than praised for creating spontaneous footy. The team endured the vocal lashings and kept fun on the field most of the time and they did win every game that year. No one mentioned to coach that they had won every game without completing every set of four tackles. Their increased fitness from the Decimator must have helped the final result but the presentation ceremony felt so much better when Alexander held up the trophy last year. The premiers held their pennants up for the photo but the only one really smiling was the coach (if you could call that serpentine smirk a smile).

Back in Five Red Tim remained as anonymous as possible. When the class began to become a little rowdy, Decimus would enforce the 'no movement rule'. Every class member had to remain silent and completely still. Any movement by a pupil would be met with fast moving chalk. Tim hated this because it was so demeaning to be a man one minute and then frozen like a statue the next.

The statue needed to remain so or it quickly became a target. Fear was tangible throughout the entire classroom and Tim's hands became clammy. Even eye movements could be judged as a law violation, so the standard pose required eyes to the front. It was inevitable that some boys would be hit as the minutes slowly ebbed away. Tim had his fair share of hits. He felt powerless in this classroom. He felt it was impossible to ever challenge this gaunt, unbending, angry man.

When Decimus was in a good mood he would compare Five Red with the classes at his previous school. "I would so prefer to be at Marcellin Brothers Randwick rather than being here at Ryde. You boys are not like my boys at Marcellin. They were so much better behaved than you. They obeyed me all the time, never talked back and I hardly ever gave them the cane. Here I have to give the cane most days, so many more times than I want to."

Tim thought, *"Why did you leave then? It sounds like bloody heaven over at Randwick"*. The thoughts didn't stop Decimus. He continued:

"Why can't you boys be better behaved? Sinners go to hell you know. Those Marcellin boys are bound for heaven and you could be too. Just obey the rules, obey what I say and all will be well."

Tim almost spoke out but kept it inside, *"Why waste your time on us fools then? We're headed to hell and we don't want you there either"*. It became a popular talking point outside of class time that Decimus may as well piss off back to

Randwick because he certainly wasn't wanted here at Ryde or anywhere else we were. The only boy that seemed to keep Decimus at Ryde was one of the boys in the front row. Robin was the sole golden boy in the class. He never got the cane, he never got tongue-lashed, and if Decimus was ever going to give out some praise then Robin was the recipient. Robin was one of the centres in the under 10s and even if he dropped an easy catch, it was never commented on by coach. It was strange to see Decimus treat one of the members of Five Red as a human being because most were only deemed worthy of being treated down the evolutionary line; baboons perhaps.

Robin wore the tag of teacher's pet and all were jealous of him. It was a label that would take on a more sinister aspect next year when the possible reasons for the special treatment would begin to emerge.

1968 was a tough year for Tim. He was always a little afraid at home because dad's explosions could occur at any time and they were on the increase. His nerves only rested when he was in his own room with the door closed. He had always been a little afraid at school too but now he was afraid at school every day. Five Red felt like purgatory preparing him for hell. The threat of the cane and other humiliating punishments populated the religious education he was receiving. God was angry like Decimus most of the time and hell sounded like it would welcome most of Five Red.

There were so many rules to learn in daily religion

classes and there seemed no end to them. Sunday masses remained as mysterious as the ancient language they so often utilized. Some masses attended by Five Red used English instead of Latin but any personal meaning remained as elusive as ever for Tim.

There was a pattern developing amongst Catholic mentors who came into his life. The light of the goodies was being overwhelmed by the darkness of the baddies. Movies back then always had the baddies losing but for Tim it was like being in the middle of the 'Magnificent Seven' movie. The good guys start getting killed one by one and the odds were stacked against them winning. Would there be enough good guys left to save the village? Would Tim be overwhelmed like the four who were killed in the movie? Hollywood baddies specialised in black attire. Why did the Marist brothers wear black robes all the time? Priests wore black all the time too, except for the Sunday dress up. All this focus on blackness could mean these mentors are really the bad guys. Whatever the case darkness is starting to seriously affect Tim's soul, which he suspected was getting blacker too.

One of his old friends from St Mary's had become an altar boy last year and it was a gig that Tim thought might solve some of the mystery surrounding Sunday. Other altar boys said there were fringe benefits too. Taste testing the wine was one reward for all their hard work. Accessing the wine wasn't simple but it had been achieved many times without discovery.

Father O'Brien was yet another daunting man in a black robe but Tim had a higher purpose in mind to make a concerted effort to understand what is going on in this ancient ceremony. Training included a weekend session in the priest's house to learn about the various responsibilities. Perhaps O'Brien didn't like to waste electricity but the day Tim attended the training room was dark. It looked like it had been prepared to shoot a scene from a horror movie. Into the shadows he went. The mood wasn't good at the start and it wasn't helped by repeated rehearsals and O'Brien's insistence that all the learners perform their duties perfectly three times in a row. Tim already knew the priest liked a drink and he wondered if that was the reason O'Brien excused himself from the room at regular intervals. Certainly he appeared jollier than any of his apprentices at the end of the session. Tim got through it all without too much tension accumulating in his heart but it was another experience with an authority figure who didn't tolerate mistakes. O'Brien roared at a boy who had made a series of errors, "Elias! That was too early. You interrupted me before I was finished!"

Elias just shrank and muttered, "Sorry father."

"If you make one more mistake, you're out of here, no more altar boy."

Elias just nodded his head in submission. Later on he made another mistake and O'Brien fulfilled his promise. One of the main roles of an altar boy was to time the ringing of the bell at just the right moment and just at the right volume three times during the mass. The sound was a sonorous moment announcing the consecration of the body of Christ. Tim began as an intern kneeling next to an experienced boy who would ring the bell. Tim thought of the instrument that struck the bell as a banger but he would need to regard it as a ringer when he gained the privilege of holding the banger/ringer himself. O'Brien would tear strips off any boy mistiming the bell tolls or maxing the volume. That was Elias' mistake and it was just in training.

When it came time for Tim's first ring it was perfect and so was his second. The third ring became a bang interrupting O'Brien's last few words of consecrating the blood. Tim was almost kicked out of the team on his first day of being seriously involved. O'Brien blasted away and Tim certainly felt like he deserved to get kicked out. However he was used to being yelled at and he hadn't wine tasted yet, so he decided to keep going for now. It was only a few weeks later when he was able to partake of the reward for services rendered. The wine did not live up to his expectations and he felt a bit sick afterward. He wondered why the other boys put up with O'Brien just for that. Alcohol escape for Tim would present itself at a later date.

He decided to chuck in his uniform because altar boying was too much like school. Tim had thought that being actively involved beyond the communion rail where all the real stuff took place would grant him some spiritual information. Closer to the altar offered the promise of being closer to the truth. All it brought was more humiliation at the hands of people who seemed no happier than himself. The figures of Decimus and O'Brien cast heavy shadows over his religious life. They confirmed for him that nasty priests, nuns and brothers were the predominant influence in the Catholic scene.

Catholic World wasn't really any different from the jungle the teachers described outside Catholic walls. Tim had overheard adult conversations referring to lots of nasty people both inside and outside the church. Liz informed Bill on one occasion, "Did you hear about the O'Loughlins?"

"No, what about the O'Loughlins Liz?"

"Well Robbie was caught with his hands in the till at work and got himself fired. It seems he has a gambling problem and a family problem."

"Yeah he's always liked the races too much."

"And he has another woman in Lane Cove who isn't Catholic and she likes the high life and a day at the races."

"Robbie is having an affair with a Lane Cove flyer? You can't be serious."

"Yes he picked her up two years ago."

"Two women for two years."

"Well it won't be two women for long because Sharna is going to take the kids and leave him."

"What about the kids, wouldn't it be better for Robbie

to leave the woman?"

"No, both of 'em can't stand being in the same room as him."

"Bloody hell!" is all Bill can think to say.

Tim thought at the time, *"Does he love either of them or both? If he hasn't sung the blues yet, I reckon he is gonna start soon."*

Yes 1968 had problems for Tim and Robbie too but it was also an era of great new music including the blues.

With dad ensconced in the outside toilet, the West morning routine included loud rock'n'roll music inside, so all could enjoy. Liz liked some of the pop songs and she didn't want to limit the joy she saw on her kids' faces as they recognised their idols' voices. Sydney radio station 2SM played all the latest hits by The Beatles, The Rolling Stones, The Who, The Hollies and even locals like Johnny O'Keefe who released a rarities record that year. Johnny was big with Tim's brothers but he worshipped The Beatles first and foremost like most kids his age. The question of who Jude was in 'Hey Jude' consumed a significant amount of playground time. Tim played his brothers' records when everyone was out and tried to work out what the lyrics were, especially on songs like The Who's hit 'Substitute'. Did it mean that everyone looks like someone they want to be but they're really someone else?

Music was becoming as important to Tim as footy. When you really listened to songs they could transport you to another place, a better place or even a cathartic place. Wherever you were, you always felt better afterward. Even the blues helped Tim feel better because he knew that there were others feeling the same way he did. Sitting on the dock of the bay wasn't yet in Tim's literal life experience but he reckoned he had been on the bay in a mind trip if nothing else. Popular music moved him in ways that church music could not. Hymns sounded irrelevant to who he was becoming. The 60s vibe spoke of love and freedom and these were ideas that were worth exploring. If missing mass wasn't a mortal sin in both the eyes of his church and his parents, he would have stopped attending Sunday services that year.

# 6<sup>TH</sup> CLASS

~

Six Red became a refuge from the storms of last year. Decimus still prowled the playground with one eye on his former pupils but his supervision was restricted to minutes, not hours of hell that had constituted class time 1968 style. Tim's new teacher was the principal of the primary school but unlike the senior principal, he was known to be kind on occasion. Brother Antonio used the cane rarely and he seemed to be concerned about the welfare of all the boys at Marist Brothers, not just his pets. He reduced the amount of homework from last year's extremes and he recognised that making mistakes can be helpful in the learning process. He didn't talk about freedom like the songsters of the day but he did once tell the boys that God loves them, a fact that had escaped the Year Five curriculum.

The Beatles sang about love a lot and they appeared to practice it by making love not war in the short films they were producing. Could all we really need be this thing love? Tim wondered, *"Is there enough of all this love they are singing about? It comes in such small quantities it must be in short supply"*. Tim knew Albert loved him, and mum sometimes, but dad and the rest of the family were not in the love hunt as far as he could see. Sam liked him but surely it wasn't love. Boys liked each other – they didn't love each other – and if they did, it was never on view in the school playgrounds. Boys were tough. They played football not tennis, and didn't sing like girls. Some boys were sopranos before their voices broke but they didn't sing like girls. Tim's soprano singing abilities were as masculine as his footy abilities … or so he thought.

Antonio was in charge of the eisteddfod at the end of the year. He was on the lookout for individual talent. Five Red music classes had required the participation of everyone being in the choir. Boys who couldn't sing well had been identified and told to shut up and look good. Those with good voices had also been identified and told to sing up and sing up loud. Some were placed on a shortlist of potential soloists. Tim was privileged to sing loud in the choir and he found himself on the shortlist and then assigned to solo work with Mrs Smit. She was impressed during his first lesson and reported to Brother Antonio, "Tim West has the best voice in his year. He has a real chance of getting a medal at the interschool eisteddfods."

Antonio replied, "Are you sure he is that good Mrs Smit?"

"Not certain but if he applies himself he can do it."

"You know we haven't received many awards recently.'

"Yes I know.'

"Do you know West is part of a premiership footy team who could win three grand finals in a row?"

"No?"

"Brother Brendan values football awards more highly than music awards."

"Does he now?"

"Yes he does, so any extra music lessons can't get in the way of footy practice or the games themselves."

"Well that will likely cause some problems but there should be enough time to get him ready."

"It would still be an honour for the school to win a music medal. Please push him Mrs Smit but not too hard."

Tim was signed up to perform at interschool eisteddfods as well as the end-of- year school show. This didn't do Tim's tough man image any good. He got a few nicknames out of this musical notoriety but no one used them to his face yet. If he were to win a music medal it was more likely to reduce his street cred than improve it but Tim was blissfully unaware of the hopes that had been pinned on him, at least for now.

Tim was a young man discovering songs like 'Come Together' by the Beatles. Hence it was something of an indignity to be given the job of singing a good morning to a little feathered friend. This exciting musical tale communicated how some lucky individual, probably a woman, greeted a bird at their window every morning.

The only bird Tim knew had been eaten by the cat next door, before he even had a chance of being properly introduced. The lyrics were more suited to female interpretation and the accompanying music may have gone back to prehistory. For Tim the song was outside his experience and he would prefer it remain that way. Many of the notes were high and very difficult to hit consistently.

He may have had the best voice in his year but he also possessed the best set of nerves. When it came time to perform on stage in front of other schools, Tim froze up and didn't hit the notes. He came last that day and Antonio's words about failure gave him some comfort. Mrs Smit was greatly disappointed because rehearsals had been excellent. Perhaps she had pushed him by rescheduling practices and complicating his life. She was glad she had never expressed to him her hopes of a medal. Tim never expected to win and was relieved he didn't have any extra work to maintain his reputation as one of the hard guys.

His reputation had already been under scrutiny because he had won the Annual Book Week Award for his drawing of a librarian handing out novels. Some of the footy boys teased him a bit about it but it was because his poster was so good. They didn't doubt his abilities as a young artist. He didn't have to defend the fact that he had drawn it. There were many other boys who recognised his ability because Tim had done it without any serious help from a school that limited art to one lesson a week! Did Michelangelo really receive funding from the Roman Catholic Church? Tim was shocked to discover in later years that Michelangelo actually did.

He was able to finally relax a bit in class with Antonio. His teacher controlled his temper and only lost it when one of the boys did something really naughty. However serious events in class could trigger an internal gut punch when Tim was not even the object of attention. Bad language was not tolerated at Marist Brothers Ryde. Antonio asked the class, "Please can you all get your homework ready to be checked?"

The class wit responded, "What will I do then Sir?"

"What do you mean Ratchet?"

"I wasn't here yesterday so I have no homework?"

"You were here yesterday, you occupied the dunce chair for one whole lesson."

"But I left early to go to the dentist and missed this class."

"You left early yesterday but I gave you the homework the day before so you had two nights to finish it."

"Oh shit I forgot."

Not only did Ratchet forget about the homework assignment, he also forgot that 'shit' is a word for the playground not the classroom. Antonio looked like he was going to explode for a moment but he controlled himself.

"We don't use such language at this school Ratchet, come to the front." Bang, bang, bang – three of the best is not as bad as six of the best but Ratchet didn't notice the difference as his hands lit up into a deep red much like Antonio's face had been beforehand.

Back home Tim learned that his favourite brother Albert was going to join the Marist Brothers. This was good news for the Marist Order because they were getting a good man but Tim wondered whether it would it be any good for Albert himself. Did he really want to live with these guys?

Tim, along with the rest of his class, had been introduced to the living quarters of the brothers as part of their religious education. The brothers slept in a small room that resembled a prison cell. They ate together and attended mass before breakfast every day. If the visit was meant to inspire boys to take on a religious vocation, it didn't work with anyone Tim spoke to. It also held absolutely no attraction for Tim himself, despite it being the most repeated theme in teacher talk at Ryde. Becoming a brother was right up there next to Jesus according to the Catholic narrative. Marriage and parenthood might be good but definitely lower down the achievement scale along with secular vocations that were clearly inferior.

Albert would eventually tell Tim about his decision. "I know it will be hard but sacrifice is part of the Christian life and I want to know God better. The discipline may stop me getting distracted from loving God. I love teaching kids and I know you think there are teachers at Ryde that need improving on. Perhaps I can."

"You're already a hundred times better than Decimus, Albert, Antonio too."

"I want to please God Tim. I want to be more like Jesus. I want my students to know Him too."

"Are you sure that Jesus is real Albert?"

"Yes Tim, otherwise I wouldn't be able to do what I am doing. Jesus loves me and He loves you too."

"Well can you introduce Jesus to the brothers at Ryde as soon as you can and help me on it too?"

"I hope I can little brother, I hope I can."

The news of Albert's decision was followed by news that the senior principal of Ryde was moving schools. Such a move was unusual to take place midterm. It was especially unusual as he was not replacing another principal but was moving into research. Couldn't the research wait till the end of the year? Apparently it could not. Brendan was moved out of Ryde into an interstate seminary and rumours circulated that he had not been a model leader in more ways than one. Under his leadership a short temper seemed part of the job descriptions at Marist Brothers Ryde. There were out of control outbursts toward both parents and teachers on the record.

The new principal, Brother Liam, was quite a contrast. He was known to smile more than once a week. He ended the morning ritual of drinking free out-of-date milk, which was supplied daily to the school. The milk may have been good long term for tooth enamel but short-term stomachs did not welcome the creamy fluid.

Liam also made an immediate good impression on Tim by rescinding the compulsory league rule. It allowed Tim to return to playing Rugby Union on Saturdays with Sam and his old St Mary's teammates.

Ambitious leadership no longer spoiled Tim's Saturdays. His new coach was one of the parents who moved back to the Union team. Last year he had been in the habit of calming down the boys after Decimus' tirades. Encouragement was his gift and the boys needed it because the Union team did not have the same quality as the league premiers. Some boys had minimal talent but a raw enthusiasm rubbed off on the good players and the combination of the two carried the team to many victories. Tim was thrilled to be back in the team with Sam and they would often spend the whole day together afterward. The afternoon included much post game thinking. Sam said, "Why did you pass the ball to Phil, you could have scored that try yourself?"

"Phil hasn't scored a try yet."

"He may have dropped it."

"Yeah he might have but we were way out in front."

"We need a good For and Against total in case we tie in the top four."

"It just felt right to pass it.'

"Was coach happy about it?"

"He didn't say anything to me."

"Only do it when we know we are gonna win."

"What about a flick pass to you some time?"

"Hey I'm different to Phil, I'm always ready."

"Sure Sam, Mr Eveready."

"Hey I'm right behind you – most of the time."

Whether they won or not didn't matter as much now. Of course they did like to win – just not at all costs. The not-so-good players all made contributions and they were able to have fun playing the game. Risky long passes, extra passes to tryless players and even the odd flick pass were all permitted in this team. All the boys could share in the fun. Such extravagance was a mortal sin in the Book of Decimus but this book was no longer part of Tim's football life. He hoped Rod was having some fun going for the three premierships. Tim knew the pressure of three in a row was affecting some of his former teammates. The league boys were still winning but some games were close. With what lay ahead in the Union finals, Tim's more relaxed approach to team success was going to be much needed.

The Eastwood District Under 11 preliminary final was against a team they had beaten twice before but somehow the referee of the game belonged to the very club they were playing. Strident protests from Ryde's coach fell on deaf ears and the official started the game. By the time the final whistle blew the score was Becraft 3 Ryde 0. Ryde lost the game but won the penalty count 11 to 0. Tim wasn't just furious after the game. During the game he had almost attacked the ref when he blew penalty number 10 against Tim for offside. Tim had just tackled Becraft's star player legally and cut off a play that could have resulted in a score. Tim was fast, he was not offside – and both the ref and the player knew it. But one of them had a whistle and truth didn't matter to him. A bully in a uniform robbed Ryde of a grand final appearance.

The referee violated the laws and spirit of the game and Tim would find it hard to respect refs from this point on. If one of them could do that so blatantly, what other bad rulings might they inflict upon Tim and his team?

Tim spoke up during the ride home from the game, "They were offside all the time. Penalties 11 to 0, that ref's a thief."

Bill replies, "It was very unfair Tim."

"Unfair, it was bloody highway robbery!"

"Don't use that word in front of your mother."

"Why not? You do." The words had just come out of his mouth.

"Look boy. If you're not careful, you are going to spend the rest of the day in your room."

"Yeah you." These words came out barely audible but somehow his dad picked them up. Artillery fire in WWII had deafened Bill's hearing but he somehow managed to catch words that were best left to fall to the ground.

Bill screamed," Nothing else outta you boy!!"

Tim spoke no more and spent perhaps the worst day of his life in his room wondering what else dad might do to him. Bill had used the strap on his older brothers but spared Tim the privilege for some unknown reason. Bill's voice and body shook with so much rage at times that Tim could freeze up without being touched. The Voice may have been more humiliating for him than any use of the strap. The screaming levels at home and at school could make Tim's heart and body literally jump. Loud noises were on the way to establishing themselves inside Tim's internal alarm system so that anything loud could trigger him and send him back to another place. Who said time travel is impossible?

The Smith brothers next door invited Tim over on the Sunday following the lost final. He was still seething about the injustice of the match but as they played chasings and Cocky Laura 123 (a tense variation of chasings where you had to beat the cocky back to home base), Tim eventually settled down and pushed the previous day to the back of his mind. Running brought release to his heart and he laughed and played with his neighbours all afternoon. Most of the Wests were happy to see him smiling again when he came in to eat dinner in front of Disneyland on TV. Donald Duck's antics enabled more laughter and Tim was able to sleep well that night unlike the night before. Luke Smith had also invited him to a sleepover next Friday night so he had something to look forward to instead of stewing over the thoughts of not playing in the grand final.

The elder Smith often slept outside in his two-man tent. Tim had slept inside the Smith house on occasion but it had been on a blow-up bed on the floor. Sleeping outside on a blow-up bed in a sleeping bag would be fun. He hadn't done it before and he looked forward to creepy stories as they would take turns to scare each other.

Count Dracula and Dr Jekyll started off the night's tales. The presenter spoke with a flashlight shining beneath the chin to enhance the fear factor. As the stories became grosser and more macabre, Luke instead suggested they do some dares. He said everyone in the house would be asleep now and he dared Tim to do a nudie run around the backyard. Tim thought twice about it but he realised he had to accept. It was a dare and he had always taken on dares. It was cold but it would be over quickly, so he stripped off and did a circuit. He then challenged Luke to do two circuits. Luke complied but then came up with the next challenge. It was running around the whole house while still in the nude. Visualising exposure to the wide world in the Smith's front yard got Tim's heart racing but he was a quick runner so it would be OK. He made it around without anyone spotting him but when he got back to the safety of the tent he realised he had a massive stiffy. Luke noticed too and he shocked Tim by suggesting an inside dare. Luke asked, "Why don't you lie down next to me and give me a big hug." He was still in the nude from his own run and he was becoming aroused as well.

Tim said, "Won't our stiffys get in the way?"

"It will be fine Tim. I've done this before and it feels

good," Luke reassured him.

"But I'm not sure about this."

"Come on Tim it's the next dare, you have to do it."

"But if it doesn't feel right it'll be quick."

Tim lay down and reached his arm around his friend's back. To Tim's surprise the feeling of being so close to his friend, skin-to-skin was both exciting and reassuring at the same time. They rubbed against each other for a long time and the pleasure Tim felt all over got him thinking later that maybe this could be love. He liked Luke but the pleasure emanating from his genitals was a revelation and it appeared to be more than just liking. They pledged to not tell anyone else about what had happened between them. It was their secret. They would sleep out more as summer approached but no one else knew that scary stories were not the only activity going on inside that tent.

Spring ended and the night of the school eisteddfod was closing in. Tim was told to greet the feathered friend again and then play the girl in 'Sixteen Going on Seventeen'. Now he was forced to dress up as a girl, as well as sing like a girl, twice on the same night. Brother Antonio waffled on as if it would be a crowning achievement in his primary school education. Perhaps Antonio was not as kind as his reputation suggested. The final exams for School Certificate would be a cinch compared to performing these songs. They made Tim feel like a girl on the inside and 'I am sixteen' required a pink dress and high heels on the outside to complete his indignity. All his family would be there including Harold, who laughed so hard when he heard about the dress, he almost died. At least most of Tim's classmates were backstage while he was performing so they could only hear him, not see him. He hoped that the approaching school holidays of six wonderful weeks would enable the majority of his classmates to forget that Tim West was ever seen in a dress.

Tim felt quite uneasy about all this feminine role-playing. Somewhere in the midst of it he felt a dose of deja vu and after the performance Ged reminded him, "Hey Tim do you remember how I used to give you my dolls to play with?"

"What are you saying Ged?"

"Back before you were born I thought you were going to be a girl. So when you were born I decided to pretend you were a girl."

"You pretended I was a girl. Aaah ..."

"I used to play with you and give you my dolls and sometimes I put you in my old dresses."

"OK. No wonder I got the girl gigs. Does anyone else know about this?

"Only family. Hasn't Harold teased you about it before now?"

"Yes but I thought he just made it up."

"Sorry Tim, real story."

"Well don't tell any of my friends or any of yours, OK?"

"Sure Tim, my lips are sealed."

Tim thought that sometimes life just had too much information. Dressed as a girl from birth, playing with dolls and now sex games with another boy and somehow feeling OK with putting make-up on. What did it all mean? Was he someone who would marry one day? Would they have babies together?

He had been to the sex information night at school with his dad this year and he learned that the penis goes into a vagina and somewhere along the line a baby is born. Dad had asked him if he had any questions afterward. *"Are you kidding?"* thought Tim, *"No more questions from me. I am still dealing with all that other information and wondering about how you and mum managed to produce me and I have no questions. My lips are sealed!"*

Tim had turned to music to settle his soul after his little chat with dad and now he did the same after the Ged conversation. Harold had suggested at concert end that Louie the Fly might need a name change to Lois the Fly, but now with his headphones firmly in place, Tim travelled to another place. He went off to 'Itchycoo Park' as The Small Faces played on and some light came back into his heart where darkness had been threatening. Tim wished he had a small face and a small body to match it at times such as this. He didn't want any attention, wanting instead to become invisible and go hide away from this life that supplied too much information. As the Beatles sang through the phones about everything being right for the boy in question, a smile began to spread across the Roger Ramjet face. The song 'She Said, She Said' reassured him that he wasn't the only sad person in the world.

As the year drew to a close even more information emerged from Marist Brothers Ryde. The size of the info was brief but the impact was massive. Brother Decimus was moving schools again. The destination was not known at this stage but speculation was rife as to why he was leaving. The Six Red wit joked, "Marcellin must have missed him so much, they wanted him back." A trainee wit added a touch of sarcasm, "We boys at Ryde are way too unrefined for Decimus."

"Yeah Decimus is too high and mighty for the likes of us," said the wit.

"I hope it's not just a rumour," added Tim.

"No it's official. Mum works in the office and Liam signed the form," stated the trainee.

"What form is that?"

"The form moving him to another school."

"What school then?"

"I dunno. The form didn't say which school but she got it ready and handed it to him and he signed it."

Tim realized out loud, "So he won't be stuffing up anyone here anymore!" Then he thought, *"He may not be stuffing up anyone anywhere if it has anything to do with Robin."*

Decimus' previous pet had already left Ryde. First Brendan, then Robin and now the Decimator himself. Robin had been a bright child at the beginning of 1968 but by the time of his departure in 1969 his appearance had changed. He stopped playing football and he never told anyone why he was leaving except to say his dad wanted to move jobs. Adults were overheard saying that something must have happened between Decimus and Robin but no details were known. Tim was just glad the playground would be free of the Decimator next year – joy! Even coming back to school from the holidays won't be as bad as usual with Decimus gone.

Tim needed part of his own development to remain secret that year. According to the catechism this development was a sin, perhaps a mortal one, but what Tim surely knew is that religion can be confusing. One day as Tim and Sam were at a park playing Forcings Back (an AFL inspired game of having to catch the ball on the full or be forced back toward your goal line), the football went deep into some bushes. As the boys foraged for the footy Sam came upon a weather-beaten magazine. The cover had a girl with her breasts uncovered on it.

The boys temporarily forgot about the footy and focused on getting the pages unstuck without destroying the pictures inside. There were more girls and more excitement as their heartbeats increased at the sight of all that female flesh. Another secret pact was made. No one else would know about this treasure they had found. Sam took it home and hid it in the bottom of his dresser. Tim would have his time with it too. Every so often they would smuggle it to the other home and for them it felt like a feast, albeit a secret one. Tim had been prepared to appreciate the female form by regularly checking out the page three girl in the afternoon papers. The Sun was delivered to home every weekday and the Daily Mirror was delivered next door. The Mirror was more revealing in their choice of images but they paled in comparison to the pages recently discovered in the bushes.

For Tim it felt a lot like the sleepovers, different to them but wonderful as well. He considered what it is to fall in love. *"I love Elizabeth Taylor and Grace Kelly and Ingrid Bergman and Marilyn Monroe and many other actresses and now I love looking at these other ladies' breasts but I don't even know their names. Do I really love them?"* When he looked at them he felt excited and accepted and somehow free but it only lasted as long as he was looking.

He thought some more, *"It can't be a sin when it feels so good. Still there has to be more to it than simply looking"*. He experienced two-way feelings in all three dimensions in his relationship with Luke, but these women he supposedly loved were in two dimensions and it was only one-way traffic. He had never heard any of these ladies speak to him personally. He remembered the love he had sometimes felt from mum. He had forgotten that he felt mum loving him more often before he went to school. Something had happened back then but it just added to the current confusion. His search for love would involve going to places he knew nothing about now ... but love would come.

# FIRST FORM

*Year Seven in contemporary parlance*

~

Secondary school had more lay teachers than brothers. Apparently there was a shortage of religious vocations in the Catholic Church in the 60s (and 70s – on and on it seems). Maybe that was why students were constantly bombarded with the message that the religious vocation really is number one. You weren't guaranteed a place in heaven by becoming a Marist brother but apparently it gave you a big head start. Tim wondered if Albert had been influenced by the ads. When they talked about it, his big brother hadn't mentioned any hopes of increasing his chances of getting into heaven. Albert was odds on favourite out of the West household even without entering the Marist Order. Tim's chances weren't likely to be improved with his increasing focus on magazines that feature topless ladies and more.

Tim's new teacher was not part of the brotherhood. Mr Warkin was an Irishman devoted to the church. His devotion had not extended to the point of preventing him from entering into marriage and subsequently father-hood. Warkin appeared to like his children who were around the same age as the members of class. He happily told stories about his family life that helped him relate to the boys at their level. However he also had a fondness for reminding his class of the Ten Commandments. Violations of the Big Ten could easily be accompanied by outbursts of intense fury. Warkin often spoke as he was applying the cane, "I hate doing this to you," he shouted. Then another application with more empty words, "But I have to do this to you," another stroke of fury, "I hate doing this, I really do!" Tim often thought, *"If you hate it so much why not stop? Why do you look like you love it? If you hate it, shut the fuck up?"*

The jovial moods of this Irish Mr Jekyll were present most of the week but Mr Hyde could show up any time. Hyde would always emerge before the weekend and that could be worse. Heaven help the sinner who got the cane on Friday afternoon after a quiet week because it seemed Mr Warkin's anger built up over that time. Canings late Friday may well have been unscheduled but nonethe-less very practical demonstrations for First Red of the reality of hell!

It wasn't just the size of the teacher temper that was causing problems for those being disciplined at Ryde. There had been an evolutionary development in the usage of the cane over the holidays. A mutation had appeared out of the blue. Mr Warkin and others were now each in possession a short, thick rubber cane. They did more damage to hands than the previous weaponry and they created more fear in the student body as a whole as well as in the one and only Tim West.

High school did at least provide many more lessons from teachers other than the designated class teacher. First Form didn't yet allow the boys to elect their own subjects but they had a variety of input from teachers who naturally had other perspectives and of course different personalities. The domination of one teacher was finished but it was a lucky dip as to whether the new ones on team were better or worse than the regulars. Music and physical education (PE) were wins for Tim. Mrs Smit took music and the school had hired a PE specialist who wore sports gear all the time and he made it a fun period nearly all the time. The academic subjects were mostly handled by Warkin and those that weren't had a temperate individual in charge with one exception. Social Studies was a subject Tim liked but his teacher Mr Sprout took an instant dislike to him. First lesson of the year Sprout spouted, "West what are you doing sitting like that?"

"Nothing Sir."

"Why aren't you sitting up straight then?"

"I am sitting up straight Sir."

"You can't be doing nothing and sitting up straight at the same time. Which one is it West?"

"Sitting up straight Sir."

"In my class you will always be sitting up straight and you will never be doing nothing! Do you hear me West?"

"Yes Sir." How could anyone avoid hearing Sprout as he was yelling it out?

"And that goes for the lot of you! Pay attention at all times in my class!"

It was a constant mystery as to why Sprout picked on Tim most lessons. Tim was paying attention when Sprout yelled at him to sit up straight. He already was sitting up straight. Sprout often would speak down to him or worse call him up the front and order him to hold out his hand. He had to be on his best behaviour or else. Tim learned to always avoid Sprout's eyes unless directly spoken to. It reduced the number of verbal interactions with his teacher because any physical connection with him inevitably produced a negative result for Tim. The only good thing about Sprout was his consistency. Tim always knew what to expect from him.

Sprout rejected Tim without any logical reason and it added to the burden of rejection he already felt from members of his family and friends. Tim coped with his feelings of rejection in various ways. He got lost in music, he ran and played whatever sport was available and sometimes he simply used his imagination. He would picture himself in hospital with some illness and his parents would come to visit him, very concerned and expressing their love for him. He often did this in bed before he went to sleep. Praying before bed didn't seem to work but dreaming did. Hollywood movies encouraged his dreaming and they were another means of dulling his hurts. Watching Elizabeth Taylor and Sophia Loren in two-piece swimsuits had caused Tim to take notice that women could qualify as one of the world's seven wonders. His sister Ged commented to the family, "Tim is now more interested in the movies I watch, than the westerns he used to rave about."

Liz added, "Yes Tim, you do seem to be interested in girls now. Do you have any new friends we don't know about?"

Tim replied, "Come on mum … what are you talking about?"

"Any girlfriends?"

"Of course not."

Ged re-enters with, "Who's your favourite movie actress then?"

(Without hesitation) "Elizabeth Taylor."

"Oh she is gorgeous Tim," exclaims Ged.

Liz mutters, "Yes she is very beautiful."

What Liz didn't know is that there were topless ladies who had gripped her son's heart even more than Elizabeth Taylor. Tim's escapist fantasies about love had taken a new turn with the magazine discovery. He was besotted by these girls. He could picture his favourites in his head and imagine that they loved him. Why else would they show him their private parts so freely? Soon the fact that this magazine existed gave Tim ideas about getting his hands on more.

One of Tim's home duties was a Wednesday visit to the newsagent to buy his mother a copy of 'The Australian Woman's Weekly'. One day when the newsagent was busy, Tim got up the courage to venture beyond all the regular mags and enter the designated adult section. His heart rate was high simply being concerned about being found out. Still he took his opportunity and saw that some of the magazines were more revealing than anything he had seen so far. Images leaped out at him and he was captivated. His heart was pumping and it got an extra jolt when the newsagent came over and asked, "Are you over the age of 12?" Tim was not in the habit of lying but he replied, "I am end of next week." It was March not July.

"You can leave now and come back to this section after your birthday. It's off limits to underaged kids."

"So it's OK after my birthday?"

"Yes, then you can pick something from this section."

"Don't tell mum about this eh." The newsagent wasn't Catholic but he knew Tim's mother.

"OK I won't." Perhaps a liberal thinker, perhaps he saw a future regular.

Tim knew from religion classes that Jewish boys were considered men at age 12 and he thought maybe that's true for him too, even if July was months away. It was hard for Tim not to go red in the face when talk of having adulterous eyes was raised in religion classes. The Sixth Commandment says "Do Not Commit Adultery".The teacher would say boys must not look at girls with lustful eyes. In Tim's mind love was at work when he looked, although the teacher's words did raise the question of whether it really was love or lust.

Another difficult development in his first year of high school was the absence of his friend Luke. Whenever Tim would want to kick a ball around after school it was only the younger Smith who was available. Luke was almost a full year older than Tim and his brother Brett told Tim that Luke was busy chasing girls. "He just comes home late all the time now – he's got a girlfriend."

"What's her name?"

"This week it's Marie."

"What – he's getting a new girlfriend every week?"

"Not every week Tim but he's had a few."

"Shit I haven't seen anyone with him. But I haven't hardly seen him at all.'

"You aren't gonna start chasing girls too are you?"

"No … I'm still into sport more than girls."

"But you're interested aren't you? You're in love with Elizabeth Taylor."

"Yeah I really stand a chance with her."

"She's already changed husbands, you could be the next one."

"Shut up Brett, you're such a dick sometimes."

"And you're a dickhead too."

"Kick the ball will ya!"

Tim had hardly seen Luke at all and when he did see him, he was different from last year. He had changed and didn't want to talk for long at all. Luke had become a friend as close to Tim as Sam, so this behaviour was very hard to take. One Saturday afternoon months later, it dawned on Tim that Luke didn't want to be his friend anymore. He pondered how this could have happened. Had their sleepouts become a problem for Luke? He was the one who started it. Their sex play never ended badly but now Luke didn't want to play at anything anymore. It wasn't that Tim wanted to fool around sexually with him, he simply wanted him to still be his friend. It was as if a dark cloud entered the West lounge room that day and Tim began to experience some of the deep sadness that could come over his mum.

Maybe Liz was sad at the exodus of her beloved children from home base. All had moved out except for Ged and Tim. Jo had married and moved to Canberra. Brendan and Bob managed to get another two Marist Brothers casualties to share a house at Marsfield. They weren't far away geographically but they didn't call home hardly at all. She may have felt some relief that Harold had taken his teasing and teamed up with some of his cronies in a flat half an hour away. She was madly proud of Albert who had taken up the call of God on his life.

The training school for the brothers was a couple of hours away at Mittagong and Albert had to sell his Mini before starting. No car meant no visiting home but relatives were allowed one visit to the novitiate each year. Liz so looked forward to seeing her son but it was all too short and when she got back from the visit, she seemed worse. There may have been something that happened whilst they visited but Liz didn't say anything. Bill simply said that Albert was finding it hard to adjust to the religious life.

Black clouds settled on the family residence more frequently. Liz became more and more disengaged from her housework and from her family. She often complained of a really bad headache but Liz often had headaches. Suddenly the week before the rugby finals she was whisked away in an ambulance. Tim had become familiar with her lack of involvement in his life but he was as shocked as everyone else both inside and outside the family that Liz had a brain problem … it was called a brain tumour.

Tim didn't know what a tumour was but someone mentioned cancer and he knew it was bad. Bill was deeply shaken because he knew something was wrong but cancer felt way too much. The tumour had to be removed or Liz would die. Bill knew the operation itself could kill her. The long odds of success were not shared widely, especially not with the kids. Bill prayed. He spoke to Albert on the phone for a long time. Albert was let in on the secret but none of his siblings were. They wondered how much of her brain would be affected in the recovery process and didn't allow thoughts of death to remain in their own brains.

Tim asked his dad, "How long will mum be in hospital?"

"I don't know Tim. It will be a long time but when she is feeling better they will release her. I hope it won't be too long."

"Is she gonna be happier when she gets out?"

"I hope so son. We will have to help her a lot. Ged is already doing a great job with the cooking."

"What can I do?"

"Maybe you can put the washing on the line now that you can reach it."

"Sure and maybe I can do cheese toast on Sunday nights. I already know how to do that."

"Sounds good Tim."

What Tim didn't know is that his home duties would keep increasing after mum came home. Liz survived the operation and recovered more quickly than the doctors expected but she had lost part of herself in the hospital. Her head had been completely shaved but it wasn't just hair that was left behind. The tumour had been fully removed but it had left a hole that wasn't physical. Her bald head was covered with a wig but you couldn't cover up the way that mum was just not the same mum as before. Her periods of depression increased post op and Tim would learn to wash, iron, mop and vacuum to help Ged who took on the bulk of the load. Ged never teased him about his gender breaking household responsibilities which could be interpreted as a return to the dolls she gave him years ago. She knew she needed the help. Bill was active too and there were only four of them still but it became a heavy load for them all.

The increased workload meant Tim had to step up into shoes that were bigger than his size but he knew they were men's size. He would develop a sense of being over-responsible for his mum and for people in general. He would increasingly feel that he himself needed to solve the problems that the world threw at him. It was especially hard for him when mum would spend most of the day in front of the TV and resist all attempts to get her moving. His mother was a problem that he had no solution for.

# SECOND FORM RED

## *No colour demotions for Tim*

~

1971 started with more family news but whether it was good or bad depended on your perspective. Albert was voluntarily leaving the Novitiate (he had been training as a novice brother) and taking up a teaching post at Kiama. Liz was devastated that he had failed to make it all the way into the Brotherhood. She had hoped it to be his lifelong vocation. Bill had heard things on the grapevine about the Brotherhood and figured Albert may well have dodged a bullet. Bill may have converted to Catholicism but he didn't believe everything his new church brand taught. Tim was glad his blood brother didn't have to wear those black tunics anymore because they represented a way of living so unlike Albert's.

Kiama was a beach resort town and the Wests had opportunities to visit Albert on weekends, combining family reunions with a day at the beach. Liz smiled much more when Albert was around and over the year she worried less about what she had understood as a religious demotion. There were a number of Liz's clan who had made a career of the ordained ministry and their parents would uphold their child's superior standing to that of ordinary church members. Liz had lost her religious bonus points amongst these relatives but she valued being with Albert more. She may have started to see that love could be superior to religious devotion.

What was most definitely good news is that Second Form students got to choose two of their subjects. Maths, English, Geography and Science were compulsory but students could choose two out of History, Commerce, French and Latin. It's not exactly an elective smorgasboard because Tim's friends at government schools had much more choice. Brett asked Tim, "You only have four electives?"

"Yes four only, but four more than last year."

"My school has about 20, only Maths and English are compulsory."

"Is Religion one of them?"

"We don't do Religion at all."

"We still have it every bloody day."

"We have Scripture on Tuesday arvo but it ain't compulsory, most of us leave before it."

"What electives is Luke doing?"

"I think he does Business Studies and Tech Dra ..."

Tim interrupts, "Tech Drawing! That's what I want to do but we don't have it."

"Yeah that's shithouse."

"You're telling me."

Realistically Tim's choices were reduced to one subject only. Latin had been enforced on the red class in First Form and Bill insisted that Tim continue in it. Commerce held absolutely zero interest for Tim but he loved History so at least he could choose that. French may have been easier than Latin but he wasn't keen on that either. Bowing down to dad was all Tim could realistically do anyway. His siblings confirmed he had to tow the paternal line. They all did the same. Out of four subjects there was only one that Tim actually wanted to do. At this point it became very clear to him that one Catholic 'doctrine' was false. It was repeatedly said by his Catholic school that they gave a better education than government schools but this was most certainly all bullshit. Every time a teacher said it Tim thought, *"Bullshit"*.

One compulsory class that had an unsuspecting edge to it was Science. It focused one whole term solely on Biology. Marist Brothers was an all male school. There were only occasional sightings of females in non-academic classes. Women were mainly understood by the bulk of the student body to be of Venusian origin and men of Martian. Hence the topic of female biology was not a familiar subject.

When the subject changed from animal physiology to the human body, it would be a comprehensive coverage.

Tim's textbook was the biggest book yet encountered in school and it had detailed illustrations. The Science teacher, Mr Black, first covered the anatomical features shared by both genders. He then tackled the male anatomy and it entailed more than just Adam's apples. The atmosphere in the room began to tense up as the female sexual differences came to the fore. Black began describing the female genitals and for the first time, he held the full attention of the whole class. At the mention of the word 'vagina' one of the front row boys groaned and promptly fainted sideways out of his chair. There were no broken teeth in this fall but it did bring the year's most exciting lesson to a disappointing conclusion. There was concern for the poor fellow who collapsed but greater concern expressed that the mystery of how female genitals worked was only half answered. The bulk of the budding biologists were frustrated that the next lesson moved on to another subject and that lesson was never completed. The boys would have to conduct their own research.

Tim knew one of the boys already had a reputation for successfully chatting up girls. "Hey Mitch, it's a shame we never finished that science lesson. It was just getting interesting."

"I don't know why Chapel had to go and faint like that?"

"Well my heart was pumping."

"Hasn't he done any of his own experiments?"

complained Mitch again.

"You mean biology experiments?"

"Yeah female biology, you gotta check things out for yourself Tim."

"So you've checked out a vagina personally, have you?"

"What you haven't?" Mitch was full of questions today.

Tim wasn't sure he wanted to continue this conversation. He added quietly, "No".

"Well let me know if you need any help."

The conversation was over and Tim wished he hadn't said anything. Mitch seemed to know what he was talking about. He had spotted him chatting up girls at the bus stop more than once. Tim still didn't know how to talk to girls his age. There were girls he saw that he liked the look of but he wondered what was going on inside those pretty heads?

There was a new girl who walked past his house most days after he got home from school. Tim would look for her and walk from one side of the house to the other to keep looking and wondering. She was older than him but had a beautiful face and she only lived four doors down from the Wests. Tim fantasied about being her boyfriend. After a few months and after Mitch's challenge he decided he would visit her house and declare his love. He did so when she answered the door and she rejected him immediately. He was never more embarrassed in all his life. Whenever he subsequently saw her in the street he would take cover and remain as invisible as possible.

His self-esteem was shattered. He never told anyone about this.

Tim was not a born leader. He had made a career of not being noticed in class. Yet somehow the election for class captain in the last term of 1971 resulted in Tim's introduction to the heady world of politics. He was voted class captain in a landslide victory that left him speech-less afterward. He hadn't asked to be captain, he made no speeches before, during or after the election, but now he had the power. Now he was the man in charge when a teacher had to take leave from the class.

One time this new power presented some real prob-lems. The teacher had failed to calm the class before he left Tim in charge. Ratchet had been rattling off witti-cisms that were causing some unrest and may have even been responsible for the teacher leaving. Tim appealed to Ratty to settle down but simply being footy mates didn't work this time. Soon Ratty was in full flight standing up and holding court. The class was laughing and carrying on when Tim spotted the new school principal coming across the playground toward his classroom. It was the replacement for Liam, Brother Felonius was his name. (Another mysterious change of principal had taken place quietly at Marist Brothers).

Tim told the whole class to quieten down, waving his arms in a downward motion. He then boldly stood up at the front commanding quiet but it had absolutely no effect at all. Ratty's holding court did not involve any form of quiet. He was misbehaving big time and as Felonius got closer, Tim panicked. He yelled at the top of his lungs, "Shut up!" Much to Tim's surprise it worked. Felonius came into the room, ignoring the silence that preceded his entry. He yelled at Tim, "Come here you animal!" Tim assumed it must be Ratty he was talking to. He yelled again and Tim recognised this was his own life at stake. He walked slowly toward him and started shaking slightly. Felonius had presence in a room. The source of that presence was debatable but the whole class recognised the reality of its power. Silence remained throughout. Felonius adjusted his volume slightly, this time directed at Ratchet, "You too – come here."

Felonius dragged them off to his office and addressed them like criminals. "That screaming was completely unacceptable. And you boy, standing on that chair carrying on like another animal, completely unacceptable." Tim was still in shock but he mumbled in defence, "Sir, I am the class captain."

Felonius looked straight at Tim, fury emanating from red eyeballs, "Well class captains don't scream like that, only animals do." Tim said no more.

"Do you have anything to say?" was directed at Ratty but he knew better than to say anything as he shook his head. Tim wondered how his scream was any different to Felonius yelling. He probably hadn't learnt about irony in English yet but he was experiencing a serious dose of it with the school principal. Tim never raised the fact that his yell actually worked, he simply took six of the best along with Ratty. Class captain and class clown alike sharing in six of the best. Tim wasn't better than Ratty he simply felt violated for behaving just like the principal behaved and being punished for it. It was around this time that Tim adopted the popular schoolyard phrase "Fuck me dead". He reflected on the injustices that this school continued to perpetrate upon him and concluded he was being fucked over and over. He may have heard Ratty use the phrase more than once that day as they trudged back to their classroom.

One weekday that brought joy to Tim was sports day. Only five periods followed by a whole afternoon playing footy, cricket or squash. The year began with cricket and Tim enjoyed himself even though he was only an average player. The really good players were representing the school. This left a smaller range of talent in the teams left behind and there were plenty of catches to take as inexperienced batters struggled to survive.

When the winter sports programme commenced irony kicked in again for Tim. The school team was coached by Mr Black. He was a man fully devoted to the majesty of rugby league alone. He completely disdained anything smelling of that foul game rugby union. The boys who played Saturday union were an underclass of footballers according to Mr Black. Tim had to make adjustments from one code to the other. One Thursday when the football went out of bounds during a game, Tim initially prepared for a lineout (lineouts only occur in union). Tim then realised it was a scrum instead and moved toward the different location and Black took good note of it all. It didn't matter that the game wasn't delayed or that Tim remembered which code he was playing, Black always brought the incident up to humiliate Tim despite the fact he was one of the best players. Training became torture, "West what the hell are you doing? Looking for a lineout again?"

"No Sir, I'm packing down in the scrum."

"You don't think it's a ruck?" yells Mr Black.

"No Sir."

"You rugby boys are all the same, you're the worst, always playing too loose."

*"League locks are loose forwards fuckwit"* (he thinks).

"You're way too loose in your head West."

Black imagined all sorts of bullshit and threw it at Tim regularly. How twisted can authority figures get in your life? This was a question that apparently had more than one answer at Ryde. More twisted tales were being revealed as the year progressed. One teacher had caned the whole Science class because one boy offended him and some boys started to laugh. Innocence didn't come into it.

Decimus had set the benchmark in twisted teachers. He came back into playground discussions late in the year. Parents had reported within hearing range that Robin's father had tried to bring charges against Decimus for events that had taken place at the school. No one knew exactly what events had taken place but another former Five Red boy had complained to Antonio about Decimus early in 1968 and nothing had been done about it. Even though the boys didn't know details they somehow felt that their jealousy of Robin had been greatly misplaced. Robin must have had the hardest year of all in Five Red. The police reportedly didn't have enough hard evidence to enable a successful prosecution so no charges were laid.

Tim thought, *"How could God let this stuff happen if He really was in charge? Did God really care about Robin? Surely Decimus must be stopped from teaching in schools?"* The evidence against the Roman Catholic God having any real love in His heart was increasing more and more in Tim's mind and heart.

Over the holidays the Wests travelled to The Entrance and stayed in a guest house for three weeks. Bill had become the manager of a small branch of an American insurance company and was earning much more than in his former days at the bank. Hence the family progressed from camping in one big tent to having three rooms shared between parents, daughters and sons. Albert came to visit for one of the weeks and he spent time with all the family who were there. He bunked in a spare bed in the male room but spent a lot of time with his mum in particular.

Tim had one of his football mates share the room and Tony introduced him to his first and last cigarette behind the sand dunes. Tim appreciated the adrenaline but not the flavour so he passed on a second fag offer. Other vices may have been creeping into his life but smoking tobacco wasn't one of them. Tim saved his breath for taking on his father in the realm of table tennis. Bill was a good player and Tim pitted his untrained talents against him and other guests. Tim won the teenage table tennis competition but it didn't have many young female spectators. In the meantime Tony won the heart of one of the female guests in the more important battle of the sexes. Tim had strengths but winning women was a weakness that he would struggle with for some time yet.

# THIRD FORM

## *Still in Red*

~

The election of a new class captain passed without incident for Tim. He had come from obscurity the previous year and now he moved back into the safety of that obscurity. Tony and other friends introduced Tim to 'Playboy' magazine along with a bundle of pornographic paperbacks and other magazines. Teenage hormones had kicked in and the boys became obsessed with the female form. The theory and practice of getting a girlfriend and then working out how far she might go was high on the agenda. For those who lacked skills in this area porn provided something of an outlet. Fantasy played a big role in all the talk and most of it was just that – talk.

Mitch worked as a lifeguard at the local pool so his stories had at least some truth to them but too many stories left Tim feeling inadequate. It was so much easier to look at women who didn't talk back and imagine what they might do together. Pornography became a problem in his life but it wouldn't be till years later that he would recognise it as such. For now it felt like it helped him and he adopted it, unaware that it was now a primary coping mechanism, along with his reliance on an increasing record collection.

Halfway through the year the need of a variety of coping mechanisms became clear when a major medical issue emerged in the West household. A family meeting was called with everyone present except Albert. Bill almost whispered across the room, "Albert is suffering from cancer, he may not have much time left." It was spoken as gently as Bill had ever uttered but it had a similar effect to that of his raging screams. Silence ensued. It was as if an ice queen had frozen the family into the exact space they each occupied. No one knew what to say. The shock was so deep and profound. Finally Liz started to cry. Everyone else was too numb, too dumbfounded to be capable of speech. After a while Bill added, "Albert and I thought that we should keep it secret, to save you all from worrying too much." Some eyes flashed upwards at that moment but no one spoke up because dad had spoken and his word was final. Eventually Jo asked, "Is he getting treatment?"

"He had radiation treatment and it slowed the cancer down but more treatment can't help anymore."

"How long has he had it?" asked Harold.

"About two years."

Jo wondered, "He said he was just feeling a bit off with

a flu bug last year."

"That was the treatment."

"Where is he now?"

"He's in Ryde Hospital. He had a turn last night."

"Why didn't he tell me? I'm older than him, I should know," Jo questioned.

Bill just looked at Jo and Jo realised that even mum didn't know about any of this till now. She went quiet. Harold looked around, picked up what was happening and even he spoke no more. Tim didn't hear any of it because he was still numb from the shock. His mind was blank and he just sat staring vaguely at nothing in the room. He saw no one, he heard no one and he felt nothing. Some time later after the meeting finished, Tim found himself in his room crying. Before he went to bed he went to his secret stash and pulled out a Playboy and searched for any love he could see in the eyes of the women pictured before him.

Visits to the hospital were short and only two at a time. Albert was pretty weak when it was Tim's turn to visit. Bill and Tim spoke quietly to Albert and he spoke softly back. Tim held his brother's hand and felt love in his hand. Meeting Albert's eyes was hard to do but when he did there was love there too. They were able to visit another two times in the next fortnight but the third visit was the last time Tim would see his beloved brother to hold his loving hand.

A few days later Tim got a message to go to the

principal's office when he was in the midst of a History lesson. He had been enjoying being lost in the safety of earlier centuries. This type of interruption had never happened to anyone else in his class before. Boys had been sent to the principal's office by teachers mid lesson for outrageous behaviour but the principal didn't interrupt a lesson requesting a boy to come immediately unless it was something serious. Tim knew he hadn't done anything bad enough to warrant such an interruption. As he walked out of the class and across the playground he began to grasp what it must be about … Albert.

It was a long walk and dark thoughts began to assail him. Sadness descended during that journey and his steps became more laboured, especially as he climbed up the steps to the office. The principal's secretary smiled at him and as he entered the darkened room; Felonius left immediately without a word. There was Tim's father looking straight at his youngest son and strangely there was now love in his eyes. Albert was gone. Bill hugged his son tightly, desperately, and there was love in the hug too. In the moment of his greatest devastation Tim discovered that his dad did love him. The anger, the fear and the neglect faded from sight and Tim knew in that moment that his father loved him deeply. His heart was comforted.

The funeral followed in a few days but Tim didn't take much notice of what was going on because numbness had surrounded him again. It was a blanket that prevented darkness from enveloping him. The oldest and youngest brothers had looked a lot like each other. Liz couldn't look at Tim without crying. She was on the road to Numbland after she finished shedding all those tears. Liz was checking out on Tim; she was checking out of life in the West household and checking out beyond its borders too. Sitting in the big chair watching TV shows like the 'Days of Our Lives' became a full-time occupation and not just during the week, but every day. Ged, Tim and Bill all pitched in to make sure the housework got done. Liz became severely depressed. She still had some spirit in her because Bill would get angry with her and Liz could bite back occasionally. One time it became a dialogue, "You stupid old man, don't tell me what to do!"

"If I don't, you don't do anything," pleaded Bill.

"You don't know anything. You can't help me."

"I know I need to eat tonight and I know the table needs setting."

"Tim can do it," cries Liz.

"I want you to do it," cries Bill.

"Don't bother me, I'm busy."

"Liz stop it," yells Bill, "I just want you to get out of the bloody chair!"

"Sorry old man, this is my life and I'm bloody living it."

And from there the yelling session wound down and variations would occur on other evenings as Bill tried to motivate his depressed wife. The upside to Liz not cooking was that the veggies were less likely to be water saturated and the chops turned into charcoal.

Sometimes Liz would stand up by herself and leave the chair but never at the behest of her beloved husband. When her mental state changed into action mode, Liz was a sight to behold. One time she not only left the house, she also left the city, deserting both places without telling anyone. Mobile phones did not exist in 1972. She caught the train to Katoomba and bought a swag of clothes that no one needed and then her emotional high began to wane.

She found herself loaded up with bags on the Katoomba railway platform that evening. The station-master noticed her waiting for an overlong time and came up to help. Liz cooperated with the stranger and gave him her phone number after she spent time recovering it from her mind's dark recesses. Bill answered the phone at home and was greatly relieved to know she was still alive. He was glad to have her back safe and sound but less impressed with the enlargement of the West wardrobe that accompanied her.

Back in 1942 Bill was overseas fighting a bigger than big war. Liz was very active back in those days and often went out with her sister while her brothers and husband were overseas. She was walking with her sister across a well marked pedestrian crossing when a speeding driver knocked them both over. *"Why wasn't he fighting overseas rather than causing accidents at home?"* thought Liz's sister as she bounced back up again fairly quickly. She had fallen less heavily than Liz who was knocked out and unconscious. Liz recovered slowly in hospital after suffering some memory loss along with a quite visibly broken arm.

After the birth of Jo in 1943 Liz suffered from post-natal depression and had no help from Bill. Her sister was having her own children and Liz learned to cope pretty much alone. Bill had come home on leave for a month and she became pregnant again. Whilst pregnant with her first son, the O'Donovans were notified of the death of her young brother Albert in Papua New Guinea. Newspapers covered the loss of this brilliant young cricketer who was destined to wear the baggy green of the Australian side. Liz was cut to the heart as she grieved the loss of her closest sibling. He was only 19. Albert was kind and loving especially to his big sister. He wasn't a great competitor, rather he was simply full of talent and gracious in acknowledging God had given it to him. Liz wept. Some of her snobby relatives turned up at the funeral because they knew her young brother would have batted one day for Australia. Instead he died for it.

Back in those days, the days of world wars and a great depression, you just toughed out the bad times, women and men alike. Liz was no doubt profoundly affected by these traumatic events. Her recent brain surgery would only have complicated her cerebral functioning, let alone the pain in her heart. Now as she faced the loss of the child she had named after her deceased brother, she descended into whereabouts unknown. Tim would only discover many years later that lithium had been prescribed for his mother. She had been diagnosed as a Manic Depressive.

From Tim's view, mum was just sad and unmotivated and he thought he must have contributed to it. Many children blame themselves when they see problems in their family. If Tim had been a better son, mum would be happy. Albert had been a good son. He wondered why Albert had been taken away. They said Lazarus was raised from the dead back in Bible days. If Jesus was real surely He could have saved Albert from dying or brought him back to life. Hope can only be held for so long.

This was the year when part of Tim floated away to another place. It was probably the same place where a big part of mum was. Sadly both were unaware of the other's presence there. Numbness became part of normal living. It would come and go and Tim learned more ways of escaping emotional torment via new music, old movies and more magazines of the adult variety. His classmates were way ahead of him in gathering increasingly pornographic material but he would soon catch up. 'Playboy' became 'Penthouse', which increased his knowledge of female anatomy but only made him feel embarrassed when he tried talking to a real girl. The girls in his area went to a couple of schools and he would see them at the bus stop waiting for the same bus that Tim caught. This provided opportunities for advancement in his ability to effectively communicate with the opposite gender but his mind was already preoccupied with recent events and he failed to advance in the battle of the sexes.

Mitch knew two of the girls that caught the bus at Tim's stop. Mitch told him how one was his current girlfriend and the other his ex. The ex was currently available and Mitch wouldn't bash him for attempting to befriend her. Tim was a man of few words but Mitch always had more words and stories to boot. Tim began to avoid the class Casanova whenever possible.

Tim really liked his ex. She was available but he hadn't even spoken to her alone yet. He had once taken a seat next to her but his heartbeat so hard he couldn't hear his own thoughts. He had smiled at her before sitting down and she had smiled back. A promising beginning then turned to nothing as his body froze, especially the Ramjet jaw. No words emerged but the mouth kept smiling while a worrying notion established itself inside his head, *"My chin is too big for her to like me"*. This lie prevented his ability to think of anything positive to say out loud. Albert had a chin like his and he never really got a serious girlfriend. Talking about Albert in any way was a no-go zone but the impact of his brother's death affected his outside world in many ways. It inhibited Tim from talking much to people in general and that included potential girlfriends.

Hollywood didn't provide much help in this area. Cary Grant was one of Ged's favourite actors and Tim often watched old movies at home with her. In the movie

'To Catch a Thief' Tim hoped to pick up some useful lines to say to Diana, the ex that got his heart racing so much that his mind became a blur. Grace Kelly would melt at some of Cary's lines and Tim knew this was just a movie but you never know perhaps it could work in real life too. Tim was still trying not to melt himself when he looked into Diana's eyes, let alone remember some corny line that might melt her.

After a number of months Mitch invited Tim to go ten pin bowling on Saturday with a mixed group, which included Diana. Tim and Mitch had been bowling for summer sport together and Tim had learned to change subjects if Mitch went on about his girlfriends for too long. Mitch said in anticipation of the weekend, "How do you think you will go with Diana on Saturday?"

"I dunno. I used to think Cary Grant had some good lines but I don't think I have the looks to back it up."

"His chin is similar to yours, just more chiseled."

"Yeah and not as big I know. How did you speak to Diana when you first met?"

"I can't reveal the secrets of my profession to amateurs," Mitch pronounced in an English accent.

"Yeah, yeah I'm just an amateur but amateur golfers become pros," came the reply in an American accent.

"I just told her I liked her and it went on from there. I'm not sure how long it was before we were kissing but she's a great kisser."

"Enough information there thanks and why did you

break up?"

"Hey that's confidential."

"Did she break it off instead of you?"

"Hey no more questions."

"Sure boss, say no more."

Tim didn't have to avoid Mitch anymore and he was learning how to guide male conversations at least. Tim and Mitch had become good friends. Tim was finally able to talk to Diana without suffering partial brain death and he didn't need to use any Cary Grant lines. Diana never became his girlfriend but she liked Tim as a friend and their relationship reduced his risk of heart attacks when meeting new girls. The absence of female students at Marist Brothers had enlarged the hurdles in the battle of the sexes but his friendship with Diana increased Tim's confidence.

Tim was excited by his progress in understanding girls but he still felt unattractive to them in some way. He didn't expect them to like him. The West chin was one thing but physical defects were less oppressive than internal ones. He felt deep down that if Diana got to know him heaps better she wouldn't like him either. The girl up the street had rejected him last year and he felt rejected by his family especially by his mother now and he had always felt alienated by Harold. Now Albert's death imposed a sense of rejection upon him too. Another negative notion formed in his mind, *"Albert didn't want to be part of my life anymore"*. Negative thinking became an all too regular part of Tim's life and at times he felt as if he was drowning in darkness. He identified with blues music so much because the songwriters were men who knew the darkness existed and how hard it could be. The song about living under a bad sign resonated within a heart that was slowly hardening.

He would retreat into his headphones listening to albums like 'Slade Alive' or 'Tommy' by The Who and attempt to leave his troubles behind for a while. Tommy had a tough life but it got better by album end and maybe Tim's could get better too. Movies like 'The French Connection' or 'Patton' provided an escape into worlds that relieved his anxious feelings. With his recent inroads into Girl World he felt too guilty to look at the magazines hidden in his dresser or go to the newsagent and buy new ones. If one of the girls spotted him buying one of those mags he would be just too embarrassed. Next year an event would disable the guilt and ramp up the mags but for now he relied on music and movies for escape.

# FOURTH FORM RED

~

The new year heralded good news. Harold was moving overseas to Hong Kong. Bill couldn't understand how his most difficult son rose in the insurance ranks so quickly. His meteoric moves up the corporate ladder were likely assisted by his years of training in deviousness in the West household. Such prodigious talent would no doubt be appreciated by some of the insurance managers he worked for. 'Citizen Kane' was one of Harold's movie heroes and he probably hoped to follow in his footsteps.

Tim luxuriated in the fact that now Harold's Chinese associates would have the pleasure of putting up with his continual teasing and pranks. Even though he had left home years before, occasional visits back home demonstrated how real Jo's warning to Bill was. Louie the Fly wasn't the only name labelled on Tim. Harold continually cast slurs upon his brother's masculinity. Now with the South China Sea between them, Tim could relax at last. Hopefully Harold wouldn't piss off his employer too much and get sent back soon.

There was more good news in the form of Tim's main teacher being a much-loved Canadian layman about whom former students raved. Mr McNulty was an even-tempered individual who smiled too much to be considered a Roman Catholic in Tim's mind. He told funny stories about playing ice hockey, which so enraptured his listeners that the summer heat in the classroom somehow lowered in temperature. Tales of Canadian operations in World War II enlivened his History class to the point in which the students felt they were hearing eyewitness testimony. He even allowed the student men before him to be real men and address him by his first name when he was off duty. Tim was turning 15 this year and he began to feel as though he really could become a man in more areas of life other than football. He had felt he had been a man on the footy field for years.

Mike McNulty represented new life for Tim. He had enjoyed a moment of true love from his father last year and here now was someone who had many moments of love to share with his pupils. It wasn't anything like the pampering that Decimus laid on Robin. It was fresh and clean, like a fresh loaf of bread just out of the oven. He sensed he didn't have to prove himself to Mike McNulty. Tim himself was worth knowing just as he was, without having to achieve anything high or mighty.

Still Fourth Form Red was a class of 40 rambunctious boys who could put a good bloke offside on occasion. Mr

McNulty did lose his temper at times and there were a few instances when he caned a boy or two. An excursion to Long Reef included the return of an illegal jar of periwinkles. It had been smuggled in the bag of the ongoing class clown – one Mr Ralph Ratchet. Three weeks after the excursion he secretly placed the jar inside the desk of one of the high achievers and removed the lid during the lunch break. Yes, the smell reached horrendous heights even before the desk lid was lifted and when the lid came up Mr McNulty blew his lid too. A tortuous silence then ensued in which McNulty was able to discern the culprit via body language alone. Ratchet got three of the best and the rest of the students watched in horror as their saintly images of Mike, the main man, began to crumble. Why does a step forward always have to be followed by two steps backward at Ryde?

Tim's image of Mike only suffered a crack at the caning but later on that year crumbling commenced when he was caught out firing a peashooter at the periwinkle victim. Tim was then on the receiving end of two hard cuts of the aforementioned cane. They hurt more than six of the best two years before because they were delivered by his hero. Mike McNulty was a teacher whom he had truly begun to trust. Tim realised it may be possible that here was yet another teacher with a large dose of Catholic darkness hidden away deep down inside.

There were another couple of teachers, who most definitely held reservoirs of darkness within. Mr Black only taught up to Second Form but he came back into Tim's life again as the under 15 cricket coach. He needed another three boys to complete his cricket team, which played in the interschool competition on Thursdays. Tim was not especially talented at cricket but Mr Black had been informed that he had once taken five wickets for zero runs in just one over. The fact the game was an unsupervised affair with zero talent in over 80 percent of the participants didn't matter. Tim was in. The fact that Tim hated Mr Black wasn't taken into consideration.

Also not taken into consideration in 1973 was the curse of the Latin class, which no sane student wanted to be in. It had been thrust upon the red class via its compulsory nature back in First Form and it continued on and on into the lives of Fourth Formers.

The Latin teacher, Mr Brathurst, was a foul-tempered man who did not tolerate any tomfoolery in his classroom. It was generally accepted that Brathurst was the culprit in the one-handed six of the best scandal in primary school. Latin was such a tedious subject that tomfoolery should have been included in the curriculum to help students get through it. Sleeping through the lesson was not allowed and practically impossible because Brathurst continually sprang surprise tests on his students. Failure in Latin tests was punishable with the cane. He was the first teacher to employ the cane as such and he used it a lot because the class was sick to death of the subject and its teacher.

It would be Tim's last year of Latin but what a year. After one test Brathurst caned all but three students in the class when the bulk of them had simply been confused. As Latin learning advanced the student had to break the grammatical rules that had been drummed into him earlier on. How could any brainwashed Catholic boy spend years learning thousands of rules including grammatical ones, only to then break them continually? Rules are set in stone in Catholic World. The only explanation of these insidious language violations was, "In advanced Latin rules can be broken. That's how it is". It was never taken into account that these boys had been thoroughly trained over and over to never disregard rules. Such levity in lawbreaking appeared so anti-Catholic to Tim that he thought Latin should be eternally banned from life altogether. Rules matter at Ryde and good luck to any student who persists in breaking them.

Rules certainly mattered to Mr Black. Tuesday cricket training after school started at 3.30pm precisely. It didn't matter to Black that Tim had a good reason to be late sometimes. Tim offered up in his defence, "Sorry Sir but I had to see Mr Benson after school about a special art project".

"A special art project, who cares about that when cricket training is on?"

"Mr Benson wrote me a note Sir," said Tim as he handed it over.

"This is what I think of your art project West," said

Black as he tore up the note.

Tim had no answer to that.

"Four laps now West and don't take too long!"

If he was late, he always had to do four laps by himself, irregardless of any valid excuse. Tuesday and Thursday afternoons became endurance sessions for Tim. Echoes of Decimus added to the experience of current derision from another man who lived up to his name. Black treated him as he did all rugby players, speaking in a condescending tone when addressing him and making fun of him whenever possible. Tim found real cricket games way too slow and boring in comparison to his sporting ethos. He valued continual motion in all sports. Formal cricket is the opposite. His fielding was often sleepy and sloppy, as his mind wandered off into thinking about footy, girls and music.

Tim disliked training itself, without Mr Black being added to the mix. One time Tim made some fielding errors and Black came at him in a massive display of vitriol, "West you are such a simpleton!" No reply from Tim.

"Why can't you pay attention? You're ... a fool!" Black avoided embellishing the accusation with the alliterated adjective but all the players recognised its unspoken presence. Tim's teammates saw it was harsh beyond any necessity. Its result was that Tim froze up for the rest of the session. His fielding did not improve with these cruel coaching tactics and Black never asked if there were any mitigating circumstances.

The reason Tim was even more off his game today was the caning he and others had received for failing another Latin test. How he hated Brathurst and Black. They hated him and he hated them back. Hate was not the only emotion they prompted inside Tim. It was more likely that fear was a deeper problem. He feared these men just as he had feared many other authority figures up till now. A small degree of anxiety or fear crept into his classes with McNulty. The repeated years of caning and verbal abuse from school and family had taken a toll.

The recent loss of Albert had probably led to an accumulation of rejection and fear inside Tim's heart that day. He needed to leave the field and make a simple visit to the toilet. As the need increased he could not call out to Black for permission to leave the field. He had fully frozen and was unable to move. The ball did not come his way but he wet his pants that day right there on the cricket field. It was just like he wet his pants at the beginning of his godforsaken schooling in this out of date institution called the Roman Catholic Church.

In an amazing display of solidarity and perhaps in mutual disrespect for their coach, the team did not rat on Tim. The wet sports pants of Tim West may have been mentioned in the staff room but the incident was never leaked to any of Tim's fellow students. It could also have been due to the fact that Tim moved in many circles at Ryde. He knew high achievers as well as middle achievers and all the sporty guys. He made friends with boys irregardless of the colour of their skin or class designation. He had been part of various groups over the years. He hung around after school avoiding going home early playing with the handball guys who also didn't want to go home. He still loved drawing and he talked to the arty types because he understood that world too. He had creds with the girlfriend group that Mitch had invited him into. All the guys he had been assigned to sit with in the twin desk system at Ryde were still friends of his in his mind, even though he didn't hang with many of them now. Tim was loyal. He even considered the peashooting victim a friend, even though it had been years since they had played together.

All these friends didn't mean that Tim was universally adored at Ryde. The previous year he had been attacked near the cricket nets when a boy from the year above him decided to start swinging punches at him. It was such a shock at the time. This boy was unknown to Tim and he never did get to know why he had attacked him but attack him he did. Tim had learned how to protect himself on the footy field, so he started swinging back. Neither of them were landing many punches but the assembling crowd aroused the attention and intervention of the teacher on duty. Both boys got caned and Tim was pretty pissed that all he had done was fight to protect himself from a crazy guy. It also didn't help his mental processing of safety factors that some random individual could suddenly try to take you out for no understandable reason. If there was a god, he just didn't seem able to preside over his creation very fairly and some of the Old Testament stories in Religion class only gave credence to that theory.

Tim asked a question in Religion class, "Why did God stop Moses from going into the promised land?"

His teacher replied, "Moses disobeyed God when he hit the rock in the desert instead of speaking to it."

"But he obeyed God in so much other stuff."

"It only takes one law to be broken for punishment to follow."

"He hit the rock instead of speaking to the rock. We get hit all the time and the teachers don't get in trouble. How is that?"

His teacher replied sternly, "Keep up that attitude West and we'll find out whether I suffer at all for hitting you." Of course Tim wasn't stupid or brave enough to speak further and his question hung in the air, unanswered.

A football accident fed the idea in Tim's mind that chaos threatened the world more than order protected it. Perhaps the ancient Titans could be released upon the world as the Greeks had once thought. Tim didn't play in the footy finals that year. In one of the last regular games he had gone low to tackle an opponent as usual but at the same moment one of his teammates hit the opponent hard up top. A knee went straight into Tim's cheek, fracturing the bone and catching part of Tim's visual anatomy in the crack. He walked home from the home ground that Thursday feeling a little dizzy and his sister found him moaning on his bed when she got home. He was done for the day and the year. Ged got him to hospital and he was operated on that week. No more football for Tim for a while.

Another part of the story is that whilst Tim was under intensive care something happened. An orderly proceeded to give him a body wash in bed. This was normal procedure except for the way in which the orderly handled his block and tackle. Tim was still groggy from the surgical medications but he came more alert when his groin area and penis underwent a soapy massage. It was so thorough and pleasurable but somehow wrong that Tim went into freeze frame again. He couldn't tell him to stop even if he wanted to and he thought he wanted to. For Tim it was a revelation that he could actually feel that much pleasure down there. It was not that he had not experienced a tantalizing wet dream or masturbated before. He just had never masturbated that way before. Tim came to rely on this as another way of escaping the ugly feelings that had been increasing in his life.

Sam was still his best friend but he never told him about the orderly or any of his really deep thoughts. They stuck to the surface of most topics but their comraderie was real. Sam complained, "Did you hear that Black went off at one of the second years yesterday and gave him six of the best?"

"Yeah it was one of the rugby union boys."

"What is it about rugby that he goes off about?"

"Mystery of life Sam, mystery of life."

"Yeah no surprises about it but why, why, why?"

"If I knew the answer to that one I would have worked out a way to get around him. He just plain hates me."

"He hates lots of people Tim."

"He is such a fuckwit, at least we don't have him in class anymore."

"Who needs Black when we already have another fuckwit for Latin."

"Yeah Ryde may be short of girls but it sure has plenty of fuckwits."

They both laughed loudly after all this and Tim would be known for having a well developed sense of black humour. They spoke long and hard to each other about their mad teachers and how they made their lives more like hell than heaven. They focused on facts not feelings as they were in the process of becoming men and men don't talk about feelings … that's what women do.

Their various male role models sure never revealed their inner feelings. Anger was freely displayed but never tolerated in response to theirs. There were double standards here but the boys were only allowed one standard and it was measured sometimes in ridiculous ways. Hair inspections during morning assemblies were still major operations. When would the boys be spared having to endure hair over the top of the collar being reported to the principal? The brothers had insisted on a short back and sides as the standard school cut since the war. They hadn't noticed that it had been dumped by the world at large for close to a decade now. Beatle mops had paved the way for heavy metal ponytails on male students at other schools but the Marist Brothers remained stuck in the dark ages where they had gained much of their theology as well (or so it seemed to most of the student body).

There was a change in schooling practice enacted by the state, which could have been left as it was. In recent years school time in NSW had been lengthened by two years with the addition of Fifth Form and then Sixth Form. The scholastic journey once finished with the School Certificate (SC) in Fourth Form. Some of Tim's siblings had finished their schooling with a SC. This qualification used to mean everything in high school but now all students were encouraged to continue into Fifth and Sixth Form because the Higher School Certificate (HSC) counts for a good job in the 70s. Bill wanted Tim to be a teacher and teachers now needed to complete the HSC.

Tim was awarded Advanced for every subject except Latin in his SC. As it turned out his olds (colloquial for parents) were fairly satisfied with the results. Thankfully Bill didn't think that Latin mattered much anymore. Tim would have liked to get access to that bit of information earlier in the year. Bill did comment somewhat gravely at one point, "The HSC is the only one that matters these days."

"Yes dad."

# HIGH SCHOOL CERTIFICATE

## *HSC*

1974 started off well with the recognition that Fifth Form students were now worthy of the respect any adult commands. The young men wore a separate, more adult uniform than the lower grades and they had free periods when they could do their own study in class or the library. Class sizes were much reduced. Some students had left to start jobs or apprenticeships but the majority stayed and now there was room for each man to be assigned their own desk. Their teachers were less imperious, most of them resembling McNulty rather than Brathurst and two were women!

Economics wasn't Tim's passion but its teacher raised passions in the classroom that weren't always easy to disguise. Mrs Payne was under 40 years of age and her looks had no connection whatsoever to her surname. She carried a mystique akin to Jane Fonda in both aura and personality. All the boys felt she was well qualified to teach any subject so they could have her for more than just Economics. Tim wasn't the only boy who fell in love with her that year. Had Mr Payne ever ventured onto the school grounds his life may have been under threat from more than one jealous lover. Tim wondered how such a woman ever got employed at Ryde. Some students were heard to say that miracles really can take place in the 20th century – Mrs Payne's presence was hard evidence.

One advantage of having less students was that classrooms could be transformed into sporting fields quickly and returned to classrooms even quicker. Indoor soccer wasn't an official school sport but Tim and his mates practiced more often than any other game in the lunch break or supposed study periods. Even when sprung by a wandering teacher, the men were simply given a verbal dressing down. Adulthood promised so much more freedom for these growing teenagers and they were slowly getting a taste of it.

The world of music opened up big time as students exchanged their favourite records. Led Zeppelin, Deep Purple, Mott the Hoople, Peter Gabriel and Neil Young were but a few of the great artists that Tim listened to. The sexual liberation of the 60s had ongoing influences in the 70s. Sexual freedom was on the airwaves and was seen as an important personal freedom in the groups that Tim hung out with. Mitch and Sam were part of a wider network that included a number of girls. The boys often referred to their female companions as 'chicks' in conversation. It didn't lessen them as equal human beings in Tim's mind but it may have had a subliminal influence.

Tim was able to feel a bit more comfortable with the girls in the group but any time he felt his heart tugging toward one, it was not reciprocated. A random visit to a friend's place last year had ended up in a spontaneous double date to a community centre where Tim had experienced his first French kiss. His mate's girlfriend had a friend who became Tim's friend for the afternoon and when they found a secluded space she had warmly responded to his one and only advance. She loved the same music as Tim and was fun to be with and Tim had hoped their liaison might be repeated in the future ... but it wasn't to be.

The memory of that kiss and the feelings that ensued were so much better than looking at pictures of naked women whom he would never meet. The trouble was that he still felt the gap between Mars and Venus if he really liked a girl or whenever he met her for the first time. His mind would go blank or thoughts race around so quickly that none of them made the distance to his mouth. He felt so frustrated when guys like Mitch just chatted on endlessly to his girlfriends as if no effort was required.

Ged was six years older than the girls Tim liked but she was no help to him in understanding women. She was a 60s chick and his friends were living in the 70s – a generation gap there as well as the fact that Ged was always busy at home. When she had completed the household chores that Liz couldn't do, she would immediately head out with no time to talk to little brother.

'Quadrophenia' had become one of Tim's favourite records. The Who sang about whether anyone could see the real me and Tim knew that the girls in his life definitely could not. He just couldn't be his normal self when he wanted to get to know someone. Mitch always talked about using opening lines on new girls but Tim simply wanted to talk beyond the surface and get to really know someone. He had a good relationship with Diana, telling her things he hadn't told anyone else, but she was never going to be his girlfriend and he wanted a girlfriend. He wanted to be loved.

Many songs on Quadrophenia were about feeling helpless and alone and needing love. Tim misunderstood one song about drowning because living in darkness was all Tim could see sometimes. The drowning wasn't about dying but about being surrounded and completely immersed in love. He recognised the connection one day as he allowed waves of love to flow over him in the final song, "Love Reign Over Me". When that song played the world seemed to be a place where love could triumph. Was it possible that all the grief and pain that had gripped his heart would one day be relieved and love take up a central place in his life?

Albums like this would help Tim process some of his pain whereas others just distracted him from the unpleasant feelings attached to his heart. Football was the same in that he processed large chunks of anger in his devastating tacking style. He also didn't feel useless as he carried the ball into heavy contact, offloading the ball and it leading to a try. He may feel like an alien most of the time but not in the rumble of rugby battle or the dreamtime of rock'n'roll.

The football field wasn't always a place of victory but it was a place of security. His teammates were alongside him and encouraged him constantly. Tim made less mistakes than his teammates. He was the most reliable and talented player on the field and the few spectators who attended the early morning games on Saturday were more likely to call out "Go Tim" than anyone else's name. Other players were always asking advice about how he tackled opponents so easily or how many hours did it take to perfect that long pass. He was the guy they all looked to when they were down by five points with five minutes to go and he was the guy who delivered more often than not. Tim had so much energy on the field because this was the most important part of his life and he relished finishing a game as the hero. He was too big for the boys to lift him onto their shoulders but he still couldn't feel his feet touching the ground. He floated off the field in a wave of euphoria, savouring the moment and later reliving it in his mind for days and days afterward.

Not all the academic subjects at Ryde were unrelated to life. Ancient History was Tim's favourite. Learning about the precariousness of life in ancient Greece and

Rome brought comfort to his 20th century persona. Tim loved tackling but he wasn't so sure he could happily impale blokes from other city states with an iron spear. He also wasn't so sure he would have lived long enough to enjoy the military retirement plan. A couple of hours of footy each week was enough to take the edge off his aggression – he never wanted anyone to die. Tim was more inclined to investigate a career in the arts than the military. He considered outdoor work seriously because he preferred the outdoors to being stuck inside all day in a classroom or office.

One of Tim's teammates, Ted, wanted to be a carpenter. There were apprenticeships available but he turned them down because his parents and teachers talked him into continuing at school, saying he could earn more money with a HSC. He did his best to get into the right frame of mind in the ensuing months, but his loathing of academic subjects was more than he could stand. Ted walked out midyear and took up an apprenticeship, which led to a very fruitful and satisfying career. At the time he was considered stupid for dropping out by most people but Ted wanted to do what he enjoyed doing and he would have been stupid not to follow his heart. He was proved right years later by his ability to make more money than many of the university graduates that had judged him back before they got their degrees. Touché Ted!

Tim was inspired by Ted's courage and he planned

to try Graphic Design after the HSC. He figured his drawing ability should be enough to satisfy the entry requirements of the course. The increasingly academic nature of his subjects did not sit well with his heart. University would only increase the theoretical nature of the subjects and he wanted to explore reality.

Tim still liked English when the books were relevant. He would have preferred a different reading list to what the syllabus dictated. Shakespeare seemed more obtuse than ancient Latin and he wondered why popular authors didn't feature more often. Sure some classics were needed but this was the 20th century and language changes over time. Tim more often read the study guides rather than actual novels. He needed extra time to attempt to understand the increasingly complicated algebraic equations that populated his Mathematics textbook. Physics and Chemistry were becoming further branches of Maths and he could have passed over both subjects. Economics was tolerable because the teacher was Mrs Payne. Asking her questions was another opportunity to understand the female mind and looking at her was always a joy.

Tim had one encounter with her that went down in the history books. He was feeling pleased with himself after scoring the winning goal in between classes and so he became a little overconfident in his attitude. He was certainly not as mentally sharp as he needed to be. Mrs Payne said, "The law of diminishing returns is easily demonstrated by someone eating donuts. The first donut eaten tastes so good. The second donut tastes good but not as good as the first. The third may not taste good at all." It was then that Tim put up his hand.

Mrs Payne acknowledged him, "Yes Timothy."

"Have you seen some boys at morning tea Mrs Payne? The third donut goes down as fast as the first."

"Yes it might go down fast but does it taste as good?"

"I'm not sure they taste it at all." Tim was smiling at his teacher.

"They aren't dogs Tim – they can taste."

"OK then, with hot cinnamon donuts – no difference – but pineapple donuts ..."

"Remember pineapple donuts in the law of diminishing returns Timothy. The third pineapple donut isn't as good. Another example could be buying clothes. As you keep shopping, over time the satisfaction goes down."

"You haven't been shopping with my mum! She just keeps going. "

"But if she keeps buying, she will get sick of it."

"What about bikinis Mrs Payne? Buying a second bikini doesn't decrease satisfaction." A few classmates laughed.

Mrs Payne's tone turns serious, "Timothy you are being silly now."

"No I'm not, I'm trying to understand this law." Tim had no idea where his words were coming from but Ratchet must have been an influence.

"Timothy West, who do you think you are?"

"I think I'm a pretty good bloke." The words came out and Tim West was immortalized as the student who was a pretty good bloke. His classmates broke up laughing and Mrs Payne saw the humour and ended the conversation amicably. She smiled as she changed the subject to the assignment due this week. Tim never lived that phrase down. He was reminded of the title many times over and more times than he wanted but at least he knew the law of diminishing returns in exams.

Fifth Form became Sixth Form and the pressure to study increased as the dreaded HSC exams approached. There would be a Trial HSC to either prepare or terrify students into study mode. Tim learned how to put together a study timetable, which allowed time for school, sport and study. Bathing and eating became almost optional. Bill's perfectionistic streak embedded in Tim's genes was part of the problem. As well the school environment continually emphasised the HSC as the most important event to ever take place in your life. So much for a first kiss or grand final win or the death of a loved one; all that matters for the rest of your life is how well you perform in the HSC.

It was ironic that one book on the syllabus was about hidden persuaders. It warned about being overly influenced by advertising themes repeated over and over. There was nothing hidden about HSC propaganda but repeated it was. Ted had been saved from its influence but Tim hunkered down because he knew his father wanted him to go to university and Tim should at least be eligible before he announced his decision to go to technical college instead. Tim didn't have time to worry about the future because schoolwork, homework and housework filled his days.

Football at least was a highlight in his final year. After losing two of their first five games in close contests, his school team went on to win the rest of their games. The last game was played on their home turf before most of the student body and Tim had a phenomenal game. They were the Marist Catholic Schools champions and the crowd kept on cheering well after the game was over. The crowd cheered later in the year for a long time as well when the students played the teachers. Sadly, Mr Black claimed he was too small to play but the students were able to smash the other teachers both on the field and on the scoreboard. Tim took out Mr Sprout and Mr Brathurst in perfectly legal but fairly ferocious tackles. Full time 38-0.

Success on the field compensated for all the head down stuff off the field and Tim took some satisfaction in being able to achieve all he undertook that year. He did well in all of his academic subjects and was eligible to do a Bachelor of Arts at Sydney University. Bill had insisted he apply for a teacher's scholarship along the way and he received that as well. Tim could bask in the glory of his achievements for a few weeks but in the end he needed to confront his father about having a somewhat different career path in mind.

# UNIVERSITY EDUCATION

### *High academia*

~

University applications had to be in before the end of the week when Tim finally got up the courage to present his case for Graphic Design. Tim's tactic was to wait till Bill was using his drawing board. Tim addressed his father in as professional a tone as he felt appropriate, "Dad, have you heard about the Graphic Design course at Randwick Technical College?"

Bill replied, "No, why would I have an interest in that?"

"Well you are such a good draughtsman, I thought that maybe you did a course when you got your drawing board back in the day." Bill often used his wooden drawing board to craft meticulous signs and cards for community events and family occasions. Perhaps Bill had never heard of gene traits being passed on downline.

Bill raised his eyebrows, "No I didn't do a course – I'm a natural."

"Maybe I'm a natural too dad."

Bill started getting suspicious, "Yes and naturals don't need to do courses."

"Randwick has the best teachers and best employment rate for designers."

"All very good for designers but you are going to be a teacher Tim."

"Are you sure that is the best career for me?"

"Of course it is. Albert was and Brendan is a great teacher. Teaching is secure and well paid and you can go to the best university in New South Wales with a teacher's scholarship, Sydney University."

"But I want to be a designer dad, you know I can draw and I'll get a job in it."

"You haven't done technical drawing. That's a prerequisite for sure and Ryde didn't focus on art. You aren't prepared."

"I've already done two line drawings for the entry test and they're good."

"What are you trying to say Tim? You won't get a job in it. Design is not a real job anyway!" Bill's volume was on the increase.

"I don't want to be a teacher!" Tim's volume increased too.

"You are going to be a great English and History teacher!" For every increase in volume Bill was able to match it and go higher.

"I want to be a designer!"

"You already have a teacher's scholarship on offer and entry to the best university in New South Wales and you are going to take it!" The wind was starting to go out of Tim as dad's words were slamming into his ears and being simultaneously written on the wall of his heart. He offered one last hope, "Can't I do what I want to do?"

"Randwick will only get you a certificate – Sydney will get you a degree. Degrees mean money and security."

"I don't care about a degree."

"I know what's best for you Tim. One day you will thank me." The conversation was over. Bill was proud of how he had chosen what was best for his son. Surely Tim would thank him when he had a few years of teaching under his belt.

Tim went to his room and slammed the door. Bill yelled out one last order, "Don't slam the door like that!"

After calming down Tim reassessed his possibilities for next year. Design is a no go but maybe he can go to Macquarie University instead of Sydney. Macquarie was close by and most of his friends from school were going to Macquarie not Sydney. He didn't care about prestige but dad did and a few days later Bill ended another debate declaring his decision so the neighbours could hear, "Sydney University!"

Instead of riding a bicycle to Macquarie Uni, Tim would have a long walk to the train station, a 40 minute train ride and then the walk through Redfern to the Arts faculty located at the other side of Sydney's extensive grounds. He had plenty of time to think along the journey about how much he didn't want to be there. There were no friends from school in the Arts faculty at Sydney. The only Ryde boys present were studying Science and he barely recognised them when they introduced themselves over lunch in the Wentworth Building, a student facility placed on the border between faculties. Tim felt so out of place amongst the Arts faculty students that these guys became friends before too long.

All course lectures he attended alone while everyone else came in groups. He didn't make any Arts friends in the first six months at all. Eventually he got to know a guy in an English tutorial who seemed as impressed as he was about being there. Wentworth didn't just have a cafeteria, it had full size snooker tables and squash courts across the road, so Tim started spending more time at Wentworth than he did at the library. He just felt so out of place and his new friend was an outsider too. Jono didn't want to be studying Arts on a teacher's scholarship either and he decided he was going to fail his first year. He wanted to play professional football as well as have a good time. They both hung out with Tim's scientific friends playing cards at lunchtime before splitting off to the snooker room or squash courts. His new friend had a mate off campus who supplied a little grass for evening entertainment. One thing Tim did learn at uni that year was the existence of Bruce Springsteen but it wasn't learnt in a lecture theatre. On hearing 'Born to Run' he was ready for just that – running away from a life that had been imposed upon him by his all-knowing father. Who needed God when you had an omniscient mortal in the house who already knew it all?

Tim had begun to hate his father. For the last few years Bill had insisted Tim do athletics during the off-season, telling him that it would increase his speed and effectiveness as a breakaway. Tim endured the monotony of sprints and middle distance, which he simply found boring. They did improve his race times and his speed to pressure opposition backlines but he resented having to be there against his will each year. As they travelled together in silence to and from the oval, their minds were active but no words came out. Tim and Bill didn't talk much at all after the tertiary decisions had been finalised. Conversation was on the wane in the West household. Liz was rarely full of chat as depression continued to outweigh the mania and Ged would leave home this year too. What was once a thriving household of numerous noisy children running around adult legs had become more like a mortuary where the living shared rooms with the dead.

The local pub on the weekends provided a stark contrast to home life. Underage men had made their debuts at the pub months before their legal entitlement and now they treated it like their home base every Friday and Saturday night. Sam, Mitch and Ratchet were there with Tim and so was Ted who had left school early. Quite a number of other blokes who Tim didn't know as well became good friends over the years to come. They had all survived Marist Brothers Ryde and there was definitely a solidarity that came with that achievement. It was time to party!

Tim didn't fancy the taste of beer during his first schooner but he never told anyone and soon he was sculling them down as happily as a seasoned drinker. Alcohol takes the edge off a hard day and Tim was on the road to developing another coping mechanism – at least it was a culturally appropriate mechanism. If you didn't like beer then a bourbon and coke or some other alcoholic mixture became your friend. The pub became a bit like the footy field for Tim – he felt like he belonged there.

It was hard at the pub from another angle because Tim had decided to play for the local under 20s rugby team on the weekend. The club had its own drinking facilities and players were expected to drink all night at the club with their teammates after the game. Tim didn't know many of the team well and he preferred the company down at the pub. He was at home on the field during the game but he was out of place in the club afterward. One of his teammates asked him one afternoon, "Hey Tim, why don't you hang out here tonight, you keep taking off early?"

"I just don't like the atmosphere in the club, the pub's so much better."

"Yeah but this is the place where you make friends to

play in the big time." His teammate was also a player of the future and he wanted Tim's help to get there.

Tim replied, "Politics is not my thing Freddy, I just want to get there by what I do on the field."

"Yep that's where it starts but getting to know the big boys can give you a hand up."

"I have a lot of good friends down at the pub and I want to hang with them, not blokes who think they are the crème de la crème."

"Yeah I know some of them have something stuck up their arse but I know you deserve to be there."

"I reckon you will get there too – probably without having to lick their arses."

"You think so? You might be right but I might have to tickle an arse or two."

Tim was over trying to make new friends at uni and he felt the same about the club. Home was just hard work and his old friends understood his family situation. They also understood his moods that could prevent him from going out sometimes. He had suffered some bouts of depression before the HSC and one or two after, and he had hidden this as well as he could. His friends noticed more than his family. He began to be a party man, needing a few drinks to help him loosen up and talk to some of the pretty girls at the pub or party afterwards.

Tim passed his four subjects that year but 'passed' was the key word. No credits or distinctions, only passes. He had done the bare minimum to get through, taking advantage of the freedom of university life, which only marked attendance at tutorials not lectures. Loud threats from his father didn't prevent the following year being even worse than the first. Tim only passed one of his three subjects and that was a miracle because he ad-libbed most of the essays in that subject with creative writing that obviously must have pleased someone.

Tim still wanted to do Graphic Design but Bill wouldn't have any of it. The Australian Labour Party had made university free for eligible people. This benefitted underpaid working families but also gave Bill a free pass to talk Tim into going back to uni to complete his degree. Bill was retiring from work soon and planned a trip around the world on an ocean liner with Liz. Tim would have to maintain his motivation by himself while they absented themselves for three whole months.

Tim was more than capable of living by himself because he had developed domestic skills from an early age. His academic skills were also well developed but motivation was required too. Tim would not be able to sustain his uni studies during the months they were away. He had felt powerless when he agreed to go back. His father's anger had rendered him voiceless so many times it had overwhelmed him again. His sister once said to him, "Whatever dad says is the go Tim. You will never win an argument with him." She was right and to date Bill had controlled his life even down to the point of sometimes choosing what jeans to buy. The good news about the overseas trip was that Tim had no argument to win now because Bill was not present to say no to Tim's decision to leave Sydney Uni for fucking ever.

Tim discontinued his degree and got a job working in a chemical factory in riding distance from home. He was young and strong and was at least partially accepted by the workers who had been there for years. His goal was to only be there for five months before his graphic course started and was glad to meet another uni dropout on the factory floor who had got a job there due to his uncle. They talked about Monty Python and girls and music while they worked and it made the time go more quickly. Tim learnt in his sweaty overalls there that he did really need qualifications to ensure he didn't spend the rest of his life inside a factory. He enjoyed the guys but not the work.

Sadly when Bill returned from overseas he persuaded Tim to yet again return to uni next year. Their deliberation together followed the pattern of defiant youth protesting but eventually getting triggered and acquiescing as numbness overwhelmed. Bill talked the university administrators into letting Tim back in even though they didn't think it was a good idea. How right was Ged. Bill could influence uni professors and Tim wondered why father hadn't considered entering politics before retirement.

Tim tucked his tail between his legs at home and took out his pain on the footy field. He played so ferociously that year that he was selected for the Junior Wallabies and played his heart out against the Junior All Blacks in a game that finished a draw thanks to Tim's solo try in the last minute of the game. After scoring he got cramps in both legs and it appeared to the fans on the sideline that he had injured himself. Bill and Liz were there as was a female friend Tim had invited to the game. As they came off the field she was the first one there to see if he was alright and his parents wondered who was this person that they had never met.

Tim had met Sherrie at the pub a few weeks before and she liked him from the start. She had come up to Tim and asked him bluntly, "Hey, aren't you one of the rugby hotshots destined for greatness?"

"Hoping for greatness is more like it."

"I've seen you play and you are good." She sounded a little tipsy.

Tim couldn't quite get where she was coming from but it might be good. "Have I passed your test have I?"

"No, I've just had a bit to drink."

"Well join us and we'll have another drink." Tim introduced himself and his friends and Sherrie called her two friends over to complete the introductions. They talked about bands they had seen or movies they wanted to check out, finding a lot in common. Tim was thrilled to have a girl who he could talk to easily but was also prepared to become more than a friend. The relationship developed quickly and they were soon sleeping together.

Bill took Liz up to Katoomba most weekends where they stayed in the home he had designed for their retirement and was so keen to move into. This left Tim to his own devices on the weekend, so Sherrie would stay overnight on Saturday and travel to the beach on Sunday to sunbake, while Tim surfed with his school buddies. It was a fantastic arrangement till Tim realised that Sherrie was still connected to her previous boyfriend. About two months in she admitted seeing him during the week and one night later she told Tim she was still in love with her ex.

The news was devastating to Tim because he was in love with Sherrie or at least he thought he was. Sherrie's admission got him thinking about his sex life thus far. It was pretty messy. He had slept with other girls before her but it was often in the midst of drunken excess when love wasn't part of the bargain. Bob Seger sang about young lovers using each other in 'Night Moves' and it had become part of his life. It was mutual lust most of the time and Tim had lost his virginity by talking a girl into the final act. They were naked in bed fooling around but she had pulled back at the last minute. He liked her but all he really wanted was to complete his first time. All his close friends were no longer virgins and he felt pressure to prove himself. He didn't love his first partner who went all the way for him and perhaps she had wanted the relationship to slow down because she liked him a lot. Tim hoped she hadn't cared for him like that, as he now faced losing Sherrie whom he cared for so much. Love and sex seemed all rolled up in a beautiful package together as Tim and Sherrie expended themselves in his bed. They had developed such a strong bond between them and now it was cracking up.

Whether it was Karma or bad luck or the hand of God, Tim was seriously hurt every time Sherrie went from Tim back to her old boyfriend and then back again. She was confused and Tim was too. Confusion became torment as she went around in circles up to the point where Tim was completely exasperated. After the third return Tim told her that if she left again then she was never to come back to him. This was to be the final time, it was the other guy or Tim. The feelings of rejection he experienced when she left him each time were too deep and Tim experienced episodes of depression. He took a couple of sick days, which enabled him to muster up the stamina to at least go to work if nowhere else. It was when he was at the bottom of this pit that suicide seemed like it could be a good idea. Tim thought it more than once but he didn't entertain it. As he emerged from the darkness, he enthusiastically drank himself silly with his friends at the pub. Better to be down at the pub than down in the pit.

Another blow came when Tim was dropped from the Junior Wallabies. There had been a change of coach who wanted a team of his own making. Tim wasn't the only one dropped for no good reason but it made no difference to how Tim felt … betrayed. Betrayed by his first girlfriend and now by the game he loved. The new coach was placed in the same category as the under 11 referee who had lied to Tim's face. Trust was available in diminishing measures in Tim's heart and he realised that even performing at the highest level guaranteed nothing. His super performance in the green and gold should have guaranteed his automatic reselection but politics had reared up and sinned against him yet again.

Tim had always enjoyed drinking to excess on the weekends but now he mixed it up with other substances. Some pub mates were into dope as well. Tim began to smoke grass during the week and then add it to drinking on the weekends. He wanted to forget about Sherrie, forget about uni, forget about home and forget about the Wallabies. Drugs and alcohol was the programme that worked for him. His factory friend had plenty of grass and his school friends had always drunk hard and long. He also became a social smoker. He was almost prepared to try anything when he was high enough.

Tim regularly got home after his parents were asleep in bed during the week and on weekends they departed for the mountains. Home then transformed into card game nights or open house parties in their absence. All of this was hidden from Bill and Liz. They could see that Tim wasn't happy but this wasn't a family that talked about such things. Tim kept his secrets and they kept theirs.

When it came time to return to university life, Tim was

highly unmotivated but able to go through the motions for three months. He hated Sydney Uni and what it represented – his failure to do what he wanted to do. Failure to be free. He came to realise in his sober times that he had absolutely no interest in finishing the degree or teaching English and History and that he was wasting time trying to obey his father. D-Day had arrived.

Tim approached his father full of focus, "Dad I am going to become a graphic designer!"

Bill replies lackadaisically, "When are you going to give up Tim?"

Tim replies immediately, "Dad, when are you going to give up?"

"I don't give up," came a more stern response.

"This time I'm not giving up either dad."

"Well you better give up because we aren't waiting around for you to do graphic design."

"I have no interest in becoming a teacher, it's all your idea."

"And the right idea it is too."

"No, it's not my idea. I'm a man now and for me, what I want, counts more than what you want." This silenced Bill for a short time as Tim had not spoken like this before.

"Yes Tim, you are a man now, but I'm still your father."

"So are you going to decide what I buy with the money I have earned?"

Bill didn't have an immediate answer again but he

eventually piped up, "Your money is yours Tim but I know one day you will be a great teacher."

"I know I will be a better graphic designer."

At this stage Liz spoke up, "Yes Tim, an excellent graphic designer." A graphic pause ensued, then Bill spit out, "It will be on your heads if it doesn't work."

"My head can handle it," whispers Tim. And then the miracle was complete. Bill shut up. Liz had given him her look and enough was enough.

Tim discontinued his degree for the second time and applied for the design course, filling in the time in between by working in a Moove milk factory. The smells were heaps better than those at the chemical plant and the workers more his age. Tim made friends with some of the boys in the factory, admiring their honesty and authenticity, which was quite different from the uni culture he had experienced. Image didn't really matter much on the floor of this factory just as it hadn't on the previous one. There were some egos about but much less than on the university lawns.

One day Tim had to keep a secret when he saw one of the blokes mixing up a batch of vanilla milk and accidentally sneeze a rather long unlisted ingredient into the batch. Tim looked away as his mate pushed the button to mix it up with the intended ingredients. They laughed about it later but it was an exception to the rule of working hard to produce as perfect a mix as possible.

Tim had been surprised to learn that a couple of his

big new mates were serious bikies. They weren't part of a gang, just loved bikes and the freedom they felt riding. If any trouble arose in a party they were the first to ensure it didn't last. Their size, obvious strength and calm manner helped keep the peace more than once. Hanging out with these guys provided a better education than being stuck in an ivory tower at Degree World.

In the meantime Bill prepared to depart once and for all from the ancestral home. He had made a deal with Brendan to hand over the house to his family of four and a half members when they moved to Katoomba. Brendan's wife was five months pregnant with their third and Tim was another mouth to feed while he completed his certificate. Tim appreciated being included in this family, a definite improvement on the previous occupying army. He no longer had to listen to his parents argue about ridiculous things nor listen to his dad's lectures on what not to do. He was free to live much more openly with Brendan but there could be no more parties at home except for kids' birthdays, which Tim joined in on – substance free. The resident uncle discovered he quite liked playing with little ones and he even enjoyed the art of settling a crying baby. He had a touch and feel which children responded to warmly.

Brendan's wife, Natalie, was kind to him and they became friends. Occasionally she had her own style of edginess from her own family origins which meant Tim could be left wondering what she was getting upset about. However she was so much better than his mum so it was a huge relief to have a home in which love was evident. There was life in the house again expunging the demons that had settled in for too long. Children's laughter brought joy to his heart and he helped entertain them as much as possible. Natalie had her hands full with mothering three daughters of her own, and Tim wouldn't be able to help much when his course began.

# GRAPHIC DESIGN CERTIFICATE

*Creative education*

~

Tim had been accepted into the certified course mainly on the strength of his stylistic line drawings, which Bill had dismissed. The teachers recognised his eye for capturing the form and essence of objects. When Tim saw some of the other students' work he was surprised that he got in because his drawings were nowhere near as sophisticated as illustrations produced by young artists long in training. Many of the students had completed years of art as a major subject whereas Tim had 35 minutes once a week.

So he pulled his head in and placed his learning cap on tightly, thrilled to be in a world where creativity continually challenged him to expand his boundaries. Tim had never heard of books like 'Lord of the Rings' or 'Dune' and was ignorant of artists like Frank Frazetta and Chris Foss who were at the top of their fields in illustrating fantasy and sci-fi book covers. He had never heard of many others but at least his love of music meant he knew Roger Dean's amazing paintings on the covers of 'Yes' albums.

Tim became as busy as he had ever been. Travel to college was longer than the university trip. An eastern suburbs bus ride came to a total of three hours each day to get to Randwick and back. He got a job cleaning Macquarie Uni's library from 4.00 - 7.00am each weekday. Classes were 10.00am - 5.00pm, followed by nights of working on assignments – due in what sometimes seemed impossible time frames. He was being trained in the skills of artwork production as well as the disciplines required to meet industry deadlines. All his teachers were currently employed in the industry and the work so practical and exciting that Tim loved it. Whereas he had struggled to write essays about stuffy Jane Austen novels, now he was happy to work overnight reproducing photographs on an artboard using any medium that helped get the right feel. Oils, watercolours, pencils, ink and drawing pens all became familiar friends in this new world that was bringing fresh life to him.

Tim had no social life during the week, just a bit on the weekend, but it didn't matter. He was exercising talents that had been dormant for too long. Football took a back seat for the first time in his life. He didn't have time to train so he played in a social comp with some mates from his early days and it was enough. *"Fuck the meatheads running the big games*" (a thought expressed by Tim more than once). He was content to explore his artistic side. One long weekend he got so entranced by the Lord of the Rings book that he read it all in three days. He simply couldn't put it down. Mitch and Sam drove him to the beach and he ignored a crisp three metre swell so he could get to see what Mordor looked like and work out if the fall of the dark lord could take place at the hands of a hobbit!

Sam said to him as he dried himself off, "Tim it's three metres out there – sometimes four, and it's breaking left and right."

"Yeah I know, I'm not blind."

"Why aren't you out there?"

"This book is the best book I have ever read."

"Yeah but read it tonight not now."

"But it's like travelling to another world Sam. Middle Earth is so real."

"Any waves in Middle Earth?"

"Waves of Orcs not water."

Sam was still getting used to this other side of Tim. "Well don't complain about the swell next week if it's crap. You missed it."

"I won't Sam. You gotta read this book."

Tim kept reading and continued in the back seat of the car on the way home. Sam wasn't so sure about reading a book that drew you in that far and he interrupted Tim's reading all the way home with wave tales from his day.

Life at college continued to excite Tim and his drawing classes took a turn when still life subjects changed to life drawing. This is code for attempting to capture the human form whilst studying nude models. The challenge of getting the pose on paper in an accurate or stylistic way meant Tim had to focus on his drawing and not the fact the model was naked. Both sexes featured as subjects so Tim got used to the normality of nudity in the drawing class especially when the subject was male.

Yet life at college wasn't always enjoyable. Tim missed his old friends and he missed Sherrie as well. The pressure was on at times with seemingly impossible deadlines. One teacher penalized him for an unfinished assignment without listening to his very legitimate reasons. This event and others like it could raise up ugly feelings as memories of his miserable school life began to surface.

Another time his studio skills teacher had praise for Tim but it didn't come across that way, telling him he was a 'pleasant' student. Others would respond to such a phrase with appreciation, whereas Tim felt insulted by it. He didn't show his real reaction to the word, instead maintaining a smile for his teacher. However there was a strange foreboding in his heart in being associated with this word. It would be some years before he would discover the reason for his odd reaction. For now he just never wanted to be called pleasant again.

## The 4.2 – 4.5 Time

It was before the advent of Tim's formal education that something happened. Something influential in determining his life course as much as any of the school incidents. Liz had struggled to placate her youngest ever since he was first stuck by a careless nurse. She could be careless too when her mind was on other things. The so-called safety pin could slip out of her control and remind young Tim of his original jab. Liz would then have to spend time calming him down before she could get another shot at this delicate operation. One day in the midst of a severe episode of detached thinking she found herself fondling his genitals. Tim calmed down. Liz was shocked to return to the present moment and realise what she had done to her son. It was a mortal sin and she vowed to never do it again.

Post-natal depression on top of a fragile mental condition places a mother at an extreme disadvantage. She has all the concerns of a loving parent but an inability to behave in the way she would really want to. Liz had noticed how effective the fondling had been. She would save it as a last resort in her battles to settle her distressed son, but against her own convictions, she did it again. It eventually became a fast and efficient exercise, which Liz rationalized as not too much of a problem. The fondling extended beyond the season of changing nappies. Tim grew used to it and thought it was just another expression of a caring mum. Liz prepared meals, produced clean clothes, tidied toys up off the floor and read books to him. The fondling was a less regular procedure but as mummy would tell him how much she loved him around the same time, his subconscious mind associated the action with love.

Tim thought it was normal to be loved by mummy in this way. However as he grew into a young boy and began to assert himself more, uncertainty entered his mind. Tim's eyes met his mother's in the midst of a calming moment one day and Tim knew there was something not quite right about what was happening between them. Liz saw the recognition in his eyes, and ending the event quickly, began to talk about how he was growing up now and changes were coming. It was strange how composed she was as she transitioned into normalizing the conclusion of this activity because Tim was going to school next year. He was such a big boy now.

Tim's growing mental awareness was incentive for Liz to get him into school early as well as the physical maturation that made him look older than he was. Liz did not want to damage her son and it was this problem, revealed to her own heart, that she knew she needed help. She saw a doctor who prescribed lithium for her condition.

Tim was a little shocked by the sudden ending of what he perceived as a loving activity. He felt a bit numb for a few days and didn't think about it. When he remembered it the following week, he approached Liz and she told him that they weren't to talk about it anymore. He knew it would be OK without it because somehow it didn't feel right any more. She told him not to say anything about it to anyone. It had always been their secret and it would stay that way. He eventually accepted that it was part of growing up and proceeded to forget about it all, as most kids do about their preschool years.

# GRAPHIC LIFE

## *Continued*

Tim began to wonder about the word 'pleasant'. Had one of his hateful school teachers used the word on him? It would be true to form for someone like Decimus to destroy the meaning of a word like 'pleasant' by saying one thing to a boy and doing a completely different thing to him. Tim knew that his school years had deformed him in some way and that home had also contributed, but at college, school appeared the major problem in his mind. He could still picture the face of Decimus contorting into a scowl that meant bad news for someone in the class – sometimes the whole class. The veins in his neck would stand out and his eyes narrow down into the hook nose forming 'v' for vengeance. Had it been Decimus or one of the other foul teachers that had despoiled the meaning of this word 'pleasant'? The question remained unanswered for now.

Second year at college followed on from the first and

Tim was able to complete assignments more quickly as his new skills consolidated. He had more time to spend with his old friends as well the new ones. The pub crowd didn't share the same conversational subjects or sensitivities as the art mob and Tim wished he could combine these two groups that he cared for. He took the opportunity to invite his pub mates to one of the college parties, but even though both mobs liked to drink hard, there was nothing else in common except for Tim himself. The night turned into a disaster when Jono started pushing Tim's project partner around. Tim untangled them and got all his old mates out of there. If Tim had some anger issues from school then he was not alone in that. Some of his school friends had shorter fuses and it could get the group into trouble at times.

Peacemaking became one of Tim's main concerns because he had seen a fight one weekend that convinced him to never start one. Two big men he didn't know were smashing into one another and a crowd gathered around too afraid to intervene and too interested to leave. Eventually one of them fell to the ground as blood flowed freely from both contestants. The standing man then started to kick the other guy in the head. This was a catalyst for some spectators to become participants by hitting anyone near them. No one moved to help the fallen fighter but someone hit his assailant over the head from behind so Tim ran to help the guy on the ground and helped him to the relative safety of the security guard who had tried to stop it. Lunacy overtook most of the combatants while Tim moved into the shadows away from the fight like other sensible people and heard about it later on the news. No deaths but numerous hospitalizations. Tim thought head kicking was as low as you can go and he was glad he had been able to get him out without attracting attention.

Life made no sense at times. Why couldn't people get on with one another? Where did people like Harold come from? Why do I feel good for a short time and then feel as if no one really cares about me? Why does a word like 'pleasant' have dark undertones for me and no one else? Questions assailed Tim's mind as he approached the end of his course but he held them in check to focus on graduating with an excellent portfolio. He would need it to get a job in his chosen occupation and he needed it to prove his father wrong in a way that was uncontestable.

Tim gave up his part-time job and cut down his socializing like he had for the HSC, but this time with enthusiasm, rather than resentment. He produced some professional items to show potential employers and was especially proud of a poster collage that cleverly combined some of his favourite movie images. He only went to two interviews because he was accepted in the second and began work in a boutique design studio in North Sydney. Now he just had to hold on to the job and continue to work professionally. Tim fantasized about what his father would say to him when he was earning more than a teacher.

# BALACLAVA ROAD

*An informal education location*

~

Now that he was a full-time member of the Australian workforce, Tim had to take mercy on his brother's family and move into his own lodgings. His school mates occupied a rundown rental in Balaclava Road about 10 minutes drive from what had been his home for all of his 23 years. He had to pay rent for the recently vacated bedroom, shop for food and pay for phone and electricity, but the advantages outweighed the disadvantages. He had a massive bedroom, which could be left as untidy as the other bedrooms there. Household chores were on a quarterly rotation and never too seriously evaluated. One housemate chose to grab the garden hose when it was his turn to clean the bathroom and considered the job done after one serious but short application of hosing that would make a fireman proud.

Tim's skills were helpful in educating this brother in internal cleaning duties but he deliberately avoided raising the standard as high as what had been expected in the West household. Tim could finally relax at home and not be careful about whom he brought home. There had been occasions when Tim had slept with a female guest at Brendan's but it was always highly uncomfortable in the hours following her departure. Now it wasn't a problem as all his old friends had abandoned their Catholic upbringing and enjoyed the relational freedom that the 60s had brought into the open.

As much as the sexual freedom brought highs it also brought lows when it was all over. Tim felt close to the girls he slept with and he wasn't sure that multiple partners was the way of the future. Sci-fi writers like Robert Heinlein anticipated worlds featuring that very pattern, as men and women alike unshackled themselves from the prudish ideas of obsolete religions. Were people still enslaved in cultural norms that were no longer relevant or did old institutions like marriage still have a useful place in modern society? Grief and guilt still had power over Tim and he wondered if there was ever going to be a girl that he could form a lasting relationship with.

Balaclava Road was not a likely environment to assist the development of a monogamous relationship but life throws unlikely scenarios as well as the more predictable ones. There was a girl who found herself asleep on the lounge room floor of that establishment ensconced in her sleeping bag after having contacted one of Tim's old friends. That individual had rung one of Tim's housemates to see if she could stay a few nights and he had said yes but neglected to inform any of his house-mates who were down at the pub. It was Friday night and after a hard week meeting short deadlines Tim had plunged into the beers for relief and didn't notice the out-stretched body on his living room floor when the boys returned from their drinking session. Tim tripped over her and the poor girl awoke startled and unsure where she was. She had arrived from the airport three hours ago having flown in from England and was tired and jet-lagged. After she explained herself everyone dispersed to their individual sleeping quarters with Lana left on the floor.

In the morning Tim was the last person up as usual and when he entered the kitchen there was Lana looking a lot like she did last night. She had just made a cup of tea. Tim grabbed his cereal and coffee and they sat down together to actually talk to one another. Lana said, "I booked a bus to get to my parents' farm near Dunedoo. It's a small town about five hours drive away."

Tim replied, "Well it's too late today for the bus isn't it?"

"Yes it is and tomorrow is Sunday."

"So the trip has to wait till Monday. What are you gonna do today?"

"I don't know, I haven't got much money so I'm not shopping all day."

"It's sunny, why not come to the beach with me."

"I might be mistaken for a white whale, I've been living with no sun in England."

"We surf at Bungan Beach, no big crowds there shouting 'Moby Dick' so you'll be fine."

"Are you sure you want me tagging along?"

"Well I can't leave you alone all day in this dump."

"It's not the Ritz but it's shelter from the storm."

"You like Dylan do you?" and so the conversation went on. The boys had left early to avoid the onshore winds in the afternoon. Tim was not into surfing as much as his housemates so he and Lana were alone chatting together as they drove along in his Holden HT. This girl had seen Bowie perform in London and knew Peter Gabriel was the former lead singer of Genesis, so they had a lot to talk about. Tim didn't have to think hard while talking to her, the conversation just flowed in a way that had only happened once or twice before.

Lana was happy to work on her suntan while Tim joined the boys in the beach break. The drive home was just as easy but Lana preferred to sleep off her fatigue rather than join them at the pub that night. Next day they repeated the beach trip and on Monday Tim gave her a lift to the bus station. Before she left Sydney Lana had to tell Tim the reason she was going home. "I left my husband behind in England … he's divorcing me. My parents don't know and I have to go tell them now face-to-face."

Tim didn't reply. He was too stunned to know

what to say.

"I'm sorry Tim, maybe I shouldn't have told you … I don't know."

Tim saw how upset she was and managed to say, "It's OK Lana – thanks for telling me." Tim really liked her but this was complicated. She thanked him for the beach trips and off to Dunedoo she went.

A few months passed and Lana reappeared in Sydney as the new housemate of two blokes Tim drank with at the pub. One of them had been a good friend of Lana's husband before he left for overseas, both having worked for the local Council. She was still in the process of being divorced and was firmly committed to not dating anyone for at least a year. Both housemates had steady girlfriends. When Tim turned up at her front door offering her a lift to the beach, she almost said no. But she liked Tim and she wanted to have new friends in Sydney even if it was a little complicated. Going to the beach is not a date and his group all hung out at Bungan including a number of girls she hoped might become friends.

It was spring when they had first gone to the beach together and they continued the practice till summer ended, becoming very good friends. Both were committed to the friendship but it began to occur to Tim that he wasn't really interested in other girls now. Lana's marriage was over so maybe now he could ask her out to a movie. He appeared at the front door again but this time to invite her to see Meryl Streep's latest movie on

Saturday night. Now it was time for Lana to be lost for words which wasn't really her style.

Tim offered, "I've heard it's a really good movie ... Meryl could get an Oscar."

Uneasy silence continued to emanate from the female end of the conversation. "We could grab a pizza before we go – you really like Italian food."

If only Tim could see the detonations going off in Lana's mind as she considered his invitation, *"What am I doing? It's too soon! I like him but do I really like him? Maybe? Not this again, nooooooo, but hang on, yes, no, yes again?"* Lana began to smile and eventually managed to say, "That would be lovely Tim."

One date turned into another and Tim discovered that Lana liked more food than just Italian. French, Hungarian and Thai restaurants all welcomed the new couple and much of their disposable income as they spent more and more time together. Cappuccinos became the only acceptable form of coffee and wine more familiar than beer as Tim continued his culinary education well beyond the realms of dusty institutions. Some of his friends grumbled that she was still married or that she must be damaged goods but he didn't see her as any more damaged than himself and he wanted to be with her more than his mates. Tim felt it could be love that was happening between them. The wonder of the first kiss at the front door was quite a few restaurants ago and now they were ready for more intimate surroundings.

Their relationship developed into stronger bonds after the divorce was finalized and Tim helped her through the uncertainty and torment of that sad event. She freely admitted she had been at fault as much as her husband and was simply glad that children had never become part of the equation. Their three years together had been largely spent working and travelling overseas. It had seemed exciting at first but it exaggerated the flaws in their relationship and he took on another relationship almost as soon as theirs fractured. He didn't want to work on it and Lana moved to another English county and then found herself in another relationship too. She returned to Australia confused with many uncertainties in her heart but keen to build a new life in her home country. This meant Sydney because Dunedoo wasn't much bigger than a backyard dunny and small towns love to gossip.

The fact that Tim had entered the plan way too early was proving to be a wonderful development. At least that is how she felt when they were together but the broken relationships back in England had left a mark. Tim also was heart sore and confused about his broken relationship with Sherrie. The pair of them had yet to process what might have been, had circumstances taken a different turn.

The pub community was less vibrant these days as various members celebrated marriages and moved into their new lives – which did not always include the pub.

Tim's move into gastronomic culture was hardest on Sam who never quite managed to get a steady girl. He would sometimes get an invite to Lana's for dinner with Tim, or catch up with him at footy, but even that was hard because Tim didn't train any more. He was only playing for fun on Saturdays and talent carried him through the lower grades without too much pain. By the time Sam and Tim started serious preparations for their trip to Central Asia they were having doubts about going. Tim said, "I'm worried about being separated from Lana for three months Sam, it just feels too long."

"Come on Tim you can't be serious, we planned this trip long before you met her."

"Yes we did but things change, plans change."

"But you are the one who hasn't been overseas and had to do it before you settle down and don't do anything exciting anymore."

"Look I do want to go but I don't want to leave her behind."

"You aren't going to invite her along are you?"

"No, I just don't want to be away that long."

"If we don't go for three months you will regret it later on."

"Maybe two months."

"Once you are over there you won't want to come back. The travel bug doesn't leave anyone alone." They planned to explore Sri Lanka in depth, surf the Maldives, camel safari in India, trek in Nepal and meditate in a Tibetan monastery. Tim replied, "I could miss the monastery – I mean we can't even get into Tibet now."

"LOOK, I have doubts about it too because you are just so obsessed with Lana. I've been your friend since kindergarten and we have dreamed of this for years! Doesn't that mean something?" Tim was struck by the strength of his friend's words and Sam added more quietly, "And we will need a rest after all the travel. Sikkim is as good as being in Tibet."

Tim gathered himself, "Yeah there are some amazing photos of it."

"And you won't be back there again quickly so let's do it all Tim!" Sam's enthusiasm for the trip outweighed Tim's reluctance, so eventually he agreed.

Lana understood the travel bug as she had been away for years and didn't want to deprive Tim of the experience. The trip to the airport departure gate was a curious mixture of excitement and sadness as Tim forced himself to release the young woman who had come to mean so much to him. Sam was full of good cheer and knew that after the tears dried a sense of adventure would get a good hold of his best mate.

# CENTRAL ASIA

*Real world education*

~

Culture shock crept up on Tim when they changed planes in Singapore. The only two whiteys on board had heads poking above the seats like submarine periscopes, which was great for maintaining cinematic vision but not for blending in. The airline menu was curry and rice or curry and rice and the menu wasn't going to change when they landed. Colombo greeted nostrils with ever increasing pungencies and challenged temperate bodies with soaring sticky temperatures. Welcome to the tropics gentlemen where rotting is quick and easy and don't forget the Aerogard. Their wild ride in a taxi on both sides of the road to a one-star hotel ended in extended negotiations about what price had been quoted earlier by both the taxi and the hotel owners. English is spoken with an air of elegance in Sri Lanka and understood by most Aussies but there are more languages than spoken ones for tourists to master in this developing nation.

It was also something of a problem when two bodies arrived in Colombo but two surfboards landed in Bangkok. They had planned to depart the capital the next day for the beaches down south rather than hassle with airline administrators for the next four days. Nodding heads don't necessarily mean yes. The boards arrived eventually but Tim's three fin wonder had been reduced to two fins on its long journey back to its master. A repair kit was assembled over a number of days but Tim had to watch Sam catch all the good waves before his board would cure long enough to be ready to ride. He didn't have the Lord of the Rings book to occupy himself on the beach but he was writing long letters to Lana instead. Tim missed her badly in the first weeks of the trip and even felt as though she had abandoned him in the way she wanted him to go the full three months. Did she care for him as much as he was feeling for her?

Sam was interested in the Hikkaduwa nightlife. Lots of European women were on holidays looking for action. Tim had no interest in what Sam was interested in; for him it was confirmation of his dedication to Lana. He had a few drinks and talked to a few ladies as Sam looked to impress them but for Tim they were platonic encounters only. In his heart he couldn't entertain any idea of infidelity even though nightlife had been an original attraction of the trip. Sam stirred Tim about it, "Hey Saint Tim – are you gonna get any action on this trip?"

"Dunno meathead – I might simply applaud your conquests."

"Tally ho Timbo, we are away for three months you know."

"I have done the maths mate."

"You really are serious about Lana."

"You're only just noticing?"

"Yeah I know but even marriages can swing these days."

"Sam and Carol and Ted and Alice sounds complicated to me."

"What's living without a challenge – especially an attractive one."

Tim spat out, "Do you remember what Sherrie did to me? Do you?"

Sam saw he was being an idiot, "OK mate ... sorry."

Tim almost said out loud but held himself in time thinking, *"I guess that's why you like brief encounters of the shallow kind, you fucking idiot!!"* His anger had become a problem. When it came out it was intense and not always related to the problem at hand. It was uncomfortably similar to his father's outbursts but what could he do? He was his father's son though he would not admit it. He also wondered about how much his mum and dad wanted him in the first place. His mother's depression may have resulted from his birth and his heart could feel the tug of the black dog as his own anger ebbed away. Thankfully the buzz of travel provided scenes to counteract these problems and instead bring smiles to his face.

One not so hot day the dynamic duo bicycled south in their board shorts to Galle where the Aussie cricket team played and it was there that they learned that surrealism is not limited to just sleeping. They were cycling around the town in their board shorts when they came across rows of school children lining both sides of the road. It was obvious that hundreds of kids were not waiting for two half naked bronzed Aussies but somehow their ride accidently caused a round of cheering from the kids. Two of the most unlikely cultural ambassadors were getting a rousing reception for simply being there. No teachers had yet been sighted as the ambassadors lapped it up with one-handed royal salutes to their adoring fans. They completed their parade as thoughts of possible pursuit and arrest entered their minds. They finished up in a dark teahouse leaving their most recent identities behind. They had a lot of laughs about it later and would tell fellow backpackers about their ambassadorial moment of glory. Les Patterson – eat your heart out.

Visits to Sri Lankan temples were part of the itinerary and they invoked responses from overseas visitors but not always as the builders intended. The bottom level of one temple contained statues in horrifying scenarios that they could only interpret as hell. The boys were surprised how much it reminded them of stories in their religion classes. They were already familiar with scenes of people being burned up or cut in half and did not go into shock like some of the stunned locals. Both Tim and Sam may have feared such unsavoury ideas of eternity deep down in their hearts but their conscious selves rejected such horrific images as being part of their future. They walked out of that temple remaining reasonably calm but angry inside that such ideas may be prevalent in Asia as well as Australia. They had hoped that eastern religions would see another way ahead than the way Decimus had taught.

Monkeys were also adept at preventing spiritual experiences taking place within temple precincts. Tim lost his lunch to a thieving monkey when leaving one temple and Sam suffered a cut on his arm when a ravenous Bombay baboon leaped at him for no obvious reason. Sam needed stitches and lots of antiseptic in the days following as the wound threatened to cut short their trip. His arm blew up like a birthday balloon and he needed to rest for a week while Tim caught up on his letter writing to Lana. He was sending a couple of letters per week as he detailed trip highlights and lowlights so he could feel that she wasn't quite so far away. He hoped she might feel as though she was with him on some part of the journey.

In Bombay he walked the streets at 2.00am to make an international phone call at the post office. It was a double-edged walk. His excitement to hear her voice was palpable as he approached the booths but the people he had to avoid as he walked on the roadway beggared belief. The people weren't begging for money … they were all asleep on the road. On both road sides and in the middle, bodies were everywhere because they had nowhere else to sleep. It was such a revelation of his Australian privileges, walking from a secure hotel room to make an easily affordable phone call. None of these people could have afforded these simple pleasures, nor were they likely to in the future. Tim and Sam had agreed that if one of them got so sick to require hospitalization then the other would get them back to an Australian hospital rather than undergo the vagaries of the Indian health system.

Indian cities were scenes of incredible contrasts. Gleaming skyscrapers that housed eminently attired businessmen were located next to shanty lots where the underclasses shoveled mud on a daily basis. Rolls Royce vehicles battled with cycle rickshaws for a space in the traffic while both avoided the holy cow chewing barley in the centre of the melee. The other world wonder of viewing the Taj Mahal, having escaped the real world marketeers who guarded the entrance. Tim was immersed in the spectacle and dilemma of such a place and wondered why he was able to visit India but most of India would never be able to visit Australia. One night after eating at a better restaurant than normal Tim blew up, "It's just not fucking fair!"

Sam had seen the mood change but didn't expect the noise level, "Hey Tim keep it down a bit mate. What's not fair?"

"Why do we get to eat at a better restaurant because

we feel like it and most people here are lucky to get a bit of rice?"

"We're Australian Tim. Our country is the lucky country."

"But these people are like us Sam. They deserve better than what they have."

"Life isn't fair Tim, even Australia isn't fair but we don't have as many people as they have here. I dunno – it's just the way it is."

"Yeah the way it is. We're lucky but they aren't."

"Our dollar is better than their rupee."

"It's about more than money."

"Yeah it is I guess, the Brits let them go at least."

"Yeah and there's the caste system."

"Not that different from the British class system."

"Yeah if we were in London we would be the untouchables I guess."

Sam put on his best upper crust English accent, "Outcasts of the empire."

Tim added his best too, "Malingerers and convicts who will never amount to anything."

It still wasn't fucking fair Tim realised but the talk allowed him to see the enormity of the backdrop to his problem. Context can make a difference to a singular thought. Tim calmed down and smiled at his best mate who understood his outbursts and helped him talk it out.

They continued up the subcontinent through rice bowls and deserts, across the mighty Ganges and up into the mountains of Sikkim where Tim hoped there would be some respite for his battered soul, and there perhaps make some sense of the inequities and iniquities he had experienced over the last two-and-a-half months. The regime of fasting and chanting and other meditative practices gave Tim some relief in that it settled his mind down to a slower pace but he still couldn't accept all that he had seen as the way it is. The bottom line for the monks' teaching seemed to be accepting the way it is. Where is the justice in that? Where is love for the common man? Tim still had a lot of questions and there were more coming.

# RETURNING HOME

~

When Tim and Lana laid eyes on each other at the airport there was love. They embraced so long that they had to pay extra at the car park. Sam knew better than to interrupt the reunion, which Tim had been babbling on about the entire trip home. Sam thought, *"Looks like this is the real thing, maybe I could do a steady thing too."* The couple seemed bound for the bedroom in Sam's mind but like Tim he was yet to learn that there were changes on the home front too.

Lana had been through a difficult time. She missed her new boyfriend more than she thought possible despite their short time together. In the empty space she reflected on her previous relationships and how good relationships had filled holes in her life. One of her work-mates, Peggy, had been telling her about how God wants to have a relationship with her. This seemed ridiculous to her at first and Lana dismissed her friend as just too needy. The hole that Tim's absence left in her ached in a way that led to her asking Peggy about this mysterious relationship. Something in Lana's heart recognised some sort of reality to God caring about her. Peggy invited her to a group that met on Wednesday nights in a friend's home. Lana thought the participants were a bit on the conservative side but she could feel their concern for her. The group came to fill some of the love gap that she felt and she began to trust what they had to say. Love really was in the air somehow in the meeting.

The group had advised Lana that if Tim really loved her then he would agree to wait till marriage before renewing their sexual relationship. Lana's first response to this behavioural change was complete disagreement. However as she reflected on past lovemaking experiences she came to see value in waiting. She knew it would be difficult for Tim to understand what she was going through. On his return she pretended to be feeling too unwell to make love on the first few nights of their reunion. Lana was preparing to convey the depth of what was happening to her without Tim getting angry and walking out on her.

She invited him to her place for a candlelit dinner. Her housemates were out and she cooked up a three course French feast aided by an expensive bottle of red. She listened intently to travel stories that hadn't made it into the correspondence as well as a few she had already heard and she bit her lip in anticipation of the announcement she had to make.

"I missed you and you missed me when you went on

your trip Tim."

Tim replied quickly, "Yes we missed each other."

Lana jumped in, "And I cried a lot – lots and lots. I thought about my marriage falling apart and the shame of it and how I want to do better than that with you."

"You already are Lana."

"Maybe but I realised that I need more than just you too. While you were away it wasn't just you I was missing. There was a hole in my heart that needed filling. And I think that God might have filled that hole." She looked into his eyes to see what words may not reach his lips. Tim didn't say anything … he was in shock. God filling holes in hearts wasn't language he was familiar with and that such an event may have happened to his soulmate, but it was too much for one earful.

Lana stuttered, "I still love you Tim."

Tim couldn't look her in the eye anymore but muttered, "God?"

"Yes I think God is real and somehow He cares about me and you."

"God cares about me, does He?"

"You don't have to believe what I believe. I am just saying that my life is changing. I don't need to smoke dope anymore but I know you probably will and that's OK."

"No grass anymore?" Tim was puzzled because it helped Lana relax and they often enjoyed a joint together. Lana had meant to leave that revelation till later on. She got back to the real subject, "What I am really trying to say to you Tim is that I don't want to make love anymore, just for now."

"Just for now?" The dope punch hurt a bit but this punch was below the belt literally. Tim threw up his hands in astonishment, "What the fuck is going on?"

Lana tried to reassure him, "It's not that I don't want to make love to you. It's just that I don't feel right about it now."

"So your headache these last few days is a hoax."

"I didn't want a fight on our first day together."

"Bloody hell Lana, I don't know what else to say."

"I was trying to lessen the blow is all." Tim remained silent. She started crying. "Say you love me."

"You serious?" Tim was pissed off. What had happened to Lana? How can you declare love for someone and not actually make love? It felt all too much for him. Tears started to emerge from his eyes too. Both were too upset to say anything for a time but they did eventually manage to hold hands across the table.

Eventually Tim was able to say that he did love her and he agreed to hang around despite the ban on sexual activity. It was a measure of the depth of their relationship that he so easily accepted these new terms without complaining about it to himself or anyone else. He wondered at times how easily he had capitulated to such an in your face change of behaviour. Perhaps miracles do happen.

The awkwardness of this arrangement gradually dissipated and they got back to enjoying each other's company for what it was – good company. Tim had been going to suggest that he move in with Lana at some stage of his return but that went on the back burner for now. Movies and restaurants and beaches were shared experiences but the pub became the domain of men only.

A distance developed between the couple that neither could put a finger on. Lana had cut her alcohol consumption without going teetotal but Tim increased his consumption and saw more of Sam and the remnant of other singles down at the pub. He pondered the difficulties of reverse culture shock more openly as he sunk one schooner of ale after another and his friends soon tired of hearing how desperate days were for the bulk of India's population. They didn't want to be reminded how much white privilege they enjoyed perhaps at the expense of others. As these ears closed to Tim's passionate perspectives, he looked to other friends who might explore the ideas he was struggling with.

Peggy became an unlikely sounding board at Lana's dinner parties. She would encourage him to keep searching for answers at a spiritual level. She wasn't a Catholic and she never really identified herself with any particular religion but some of the things she said made real sense. Her words brought to mind the only subject Tim had liked at uni – psychology. Personality theories had resonated with his heart in ways that statistics did not. Carl Rogers and Carl Gustavus Jung described in detail real events with which Tim identified. Jung in particular was prepared to consider the spiritual dimension in life when Freud was afraid of ridicule from those who considered it an anachronistic approach. Such a brilliant mind as Jung reporting the reality of the spiritual realm helped free Tim's mind from the limitations of modernity.

He felt an internal compulsion. It may have started in the mystifying experiences in the mountain temple or perhaps earlier in India by seeing the overwhelming poverty. Tim wanted to know the truth about life. He couldn't simply upgrade his design career, buy a house, have kids and live happily ever after on a retirement plan aged 60. There was more to life than the Australian dream and Catholicism wasn't the only spiritual option in the world despite their desperate claims otherwise.

Tim began to see spiritual possibilities in areas he had never considered. Rock music had all sorts of spiritual manifestations. The Beatles sang about love well beyond the mere materialistic level. His favourite Who album, 'Quadrophenia' distinguished the difference between the head and the heart. The mind was not the only form of consciousness. Films about life beyond the physical were as numerous as Hollywood action movies. Spiritual senses could be engaged as well as the five physical ones, if life was to be lived at the fullest. Bob Dylan and Van Morrison sang about multiple forms of mystical experiences. Lyricists strained as much as poets to describe the indescribable. Jung recognised there was a realm where a lurking evil sought our embrace as well as a light that would never go out leaving us to our doom. New metaphors began to take shape in Tim's heart and perhaps they could replace the dominant themes of his childhood.

Middle Earth was not as far removed from Planet Earth when Tim reread 'The Lord of the Rings'. Light and darkness and the greys in between became clearer as he viewed the world through a different filter. Gandalf wasn't just a wizard but a son of the Light and that light may not be a fiction. There was a struggle going on in Tim's heart as he strained to believe that there really was an immaterial force in the world that actually cared for him as Lana had said. She herself was evidence for the existence of that force because of the way she had changed. The shame, which had clung to her, ebbed away and she no longer shrunk inside at the thought of being a divorcee. She was confident to do things she would not have dared to before. She would stand up to her boss and say no, whereas before she would easily submit to unfair requests for fear of losing her job. She remained employed despite the ever-increasing number of noes she uttered at work!

Meanwhile Tim marveled at how his cynical world view was on the decrease and there was often a lightness in his heart rather than the weight of the black dog. Lana was good medicine for him even without the sex and he began to realise that a marriage proposal could be in order. He posed the idea to Sam, "I think I might be ready to pop the question to Lana."

"I thought you were ready when we got back from the trip."

"I was just thinking of moving in together then."

"Yeah well that's the question isn't it? You can't be thinking of a Catholic question, can you?

"No not Catholic but I am thinking of a wedding in the park."

"Shit Tim, whatever happened to staying close to the edge. You're becoming an old man!" Sam was surprised at the strength of his feelings about such things and gave Tim a puzzled look, which took the wind out of Tim's frustration with his friend. Tim knew that Sam's parents didn't get on any more but were more committed to Catholicism than they were to each other. They remained stuck together making the family abode a constant state of misery for all its inhabitants. Sam still lived there.

Tim breathed out slowly, "Yes I know it's old fashioned but Lana has a faith life now and I can't ignore it completely."

"Yes she has faith now, I hope she has some faith in you and not just God."

Sam hadn't found any spiritual life in Sikkim nor back home and he was a little irritated at how his best friend was losing faith in the life they had always lived. Tim gave up smoking pot and lately was giving up on pub life too. He was off looking into ancient mysteries and modern psychology and philosophy and even the Bible got a look-in. Sam had forgotten that Ancient History at

Sydney Uni had taught Tim that the Bible was the most reliable source of all the ancient texts. Much of it was corroborated by archaeologists in the past and the present. Tim had not tossed his Bible away, while Sam's was probably in molten form by now at the Marsfield rubbish tip. Sam asked, "Are you enjoying your Bible reading?"

"Come on Sam I'm not just reading the Bible, there's so many good books I want to check out. I need to find answers that make sense to me." Tim was stuck on how much suffering he now saw in the world. Reading about the Vietnam conflict (war was never declared), the criminality of Nixon's administration and about the varying levels of police corruption in New South Wales … all had a profound effect on him. US foreign policy was about power and dollars not at all about saving lives and Australia was going down the same path. The Gillies Report on TV was a mirror being held up to the Australian political scene and The National Times was the only newspaper worth reading all over. Looking for truth was a big task and Tim's mental state was challenged by the state of the world in the 20th century as well as by the barbarity he read in the Old Testament. Where was God in all of this?

"Have you found any sensible answers yet?"

"I believe that God has to exist but I'm not sure about God's intentions."

"I hope you haven't found any evidence of hell.'

"No I reckon God is good but I keep getting stuck on

all the suffering."

"And do you still get struck by the black dog?"

"Yeah not often but I'm not reading all the time you know. Don't tell Lana about it."

Sometimes Tim felt that even Sam and Lana didn't really care about him. A switch went off in his mind or heart and he felt lost and abandoned again. He was able to hide it more easily these days but it was a real battle to hold himself together in front of Lana. She hadn't met his parents yet and he wasn't sure what she would think of a family with a manic depressive mother. In fact none of the girls he liked had ever been introduced to the family.

He felt his family didn't like him much so they probably wouldn't like his choice of girlfriend especially if she wasn't Catholic. Liz only married his dad after he became a member of the one true church. Tim had forsaken the Catholic church and was a member of truth seekers in general and he still wasn't sure exactly what mob Lana had become a part of. All he could get out of her was that it was a house church. It was probably unregistered and uncredentialed like his own group and that wouldn't cut mustard at home. Tim didn't even visit Brendan and Natalie anymore and was glad his parents lived a couple of hours away in the mountains.

Whatever Lana's group was called, she was going away for a weekend with Peggy and most of their group. They were attending a spiritual transformation conference, which Tim was apparently not ready for. Perhaps

Lana cared more for Peggy than she did for him. Such were the thoughts that entered his mind with an appearance of credibility. The conference was a red rag to Tim who protested his spiritual life was just as good as theirs.

Mitch rang Tim after hearing Lana was away for the coming weekend. Mitch always had more than one girl on his mind and was somehow able to keep at least two of them happy. He invited Tim on a weekend trip to Avoca with his main girlfriend and one of her girlfriends, who was having major doubts about the bloke she called a boyfriend. She had taken a shine to Tim when they had met at a recent party and he had enjoyed hearing her tales because she had also been to India.

Mitch liked playing games of strip poker on his weekends away so Tim knew it would be hard to resist such a suggestion over the length of a whole weekend. He turned Mitch down but he couldn't admit the real reason why, so he played the sick card. Whenever the black dog had raised its head just before an event, Tim often complained of being sick to his friends, so Mitch accepted the turn down as a regular part of his friendship with Tim. For Tim it was tempting to run away and relieve his feelings of being rejected in this way but he wouldn't be able to look Lana in the eye the following week if spent so much time with another girl.

Tim's trip away for three months had presumed a loving return to Lana's bed. His testosterone and unmet desire were at high levels but he was unable to dislodge his will to remain faithful to Lana. After her weekend away he continued the fake sickness so Mitch wouldn't stir him up about what he had missed. More importantly Tim had been talking to Sam about marrying Lana and he realised he didn't much care what Mitch thought about monogamy. The strength of his commitment to faithfulness was evidence of the deep connection he had with Lana, so he decided to propose soon, thereby publicly declaring his love for her. No more trips with Mitch and no infidelity for him!

Tim booked a table at the restaurant at the top of Australia Square, then Sydney's tallest tower and fitted out with a rotating floor, which showcased the city lights in all their glory. Lana knew such a location was about more than the view. He put the question to Lana and she graciously accepted against the advice of her spiritual mentors. The mentors thought the marriage may imperil Lana's faith journey but they didn't understand the depth of Tim's own journey, which looked different but was just as real. Tim hadn't yet bought a ring as he recognised shopping together would produce a better result than relying solely on his unsophisticated opinion. The couple enjoyed finding a simple but elegant ring together.

They also planned the wedding ceremony and reception. Lana had already experienced all the frills on her first wedding day so this time it would be simple but elegant like her ring. Lana's cousin was a minister so he would preside over the ceremony in a chapel but the vows were de-christianised so both Lana and Tim could make them without compromise. The cousin had different views to both Lana and Tim but allowed them space to express themselves in what was true to them. Lana was pretty sure she identified with Christ but definitely not with Christianity and Tim identified with God but wasn't sure if Christ was in any way connected. Tim had really wanted a park for the ceremony but at least the reception would be held in a relative's massive backyard. Informality was Tim's calling card and it was to take an especially informal turn on the wedding day itself.

# MARRIAGE &
# PARENTING

*Penultimate education*

~

Sam was best man and Mitch an active groomsman looking after Tim on the morning of the big day. Mitch's parents had a pool in their backyard. His place had become a bit of a hangout at the end of extra hot beach days. When 40 degree temperatures were predicted what better way to prepare for donning a suit than a game of pool volleyball. The boys were at it for over an hour when Mitch's mum called out, "Game over!" and they dried off, dressed and raced off to the chapel.

As they stood at the front of the church waiting for Lana to make her entrance, Sam informed Tim that Mitch had written 'HELP ME' on the bottom of his shoes. This was somewhat disturbing news because the couple had decided to kneel down to make their vows. Tim started sweating even more than he already was. He knew Mitch could be only stirring but anything was possible with that bloke.

The shoes were clean, the ceremony came off without a hitch and the families were happy. The reception was only difficult for Tim who hated public speaking so he sweated some more till it was over. It wasn't just anxiety that was causing sweat, it peaked at 42 degrees Celsius that day and to finish the afternoon properly, bride and groom detoured to Mitch's for more pool games before making a somewhat soggy entrance into the hotel they had booked for the night. Their suite featured an over-head mirror and the lovemaking was all that they had hoped for as they enjoyed each other after months and months of abstinence. The honeymoon was a casual trip down the south coast with spontaneous stopovers through to Melbourne and climaxing in a week at Lorne on Great Ocean Road. Australia is a beautiful country and they were loving the freedom they felt on the open road as well as the spirit of the land.

Married life was easier than Tim had anticipated in those honeymoon days. As they both settled down into regular jobs again, stresses and strains resurfaced as they acclimatised to being around each other nearly all the time. Tim's portable black and white TV rested on an inverted cardboard box, after it had been emptied of its many books. Lana suggested, "A small table might be more appropriate than a cardboard box Tim." He replied, "The last box I used lasted over a year and this one is new."

"But it's a cardboard box Tim."

"Yes that is what it is."

"It looks terrible."

"But it works and I'm sure it has many more months of service to come."

"It looks ridiculous, what will our friends say when they visit?"

"They can say what they like. Cardboard is one of the main building materials in India." Tim gave Lana a frosty look that indicated this was non-negotiable. The debate ended but it didn't do much for marital relations. There was no lovemaking that night. Tim's principles could be held so tightly to his chest that he couldn't see validity in other ideas. Gradually they engaged in more cardboard conversations and he began to realise that Lana was a homemaker as well as a great salesperson. He recognised that the homemaker in her wanted an Australian home not an Indian one. Cardboard wasn't generally on display in Aussie homes. She bought a small table for the TV without any complaint from him.

Tim compensated this break from simple living by volunteering at the local soup kitchen. He still felt guilty about living in his country of birth even though it could be considered his birthright. Tim was reading John Pilger and thought the indigenous Aussies whose land had been stolen were worthy of that birthright, not him.

Helping the homeless and other Aussie battlers helped him feel better about himself some of the time. It didn't help when struggling patrons of the soup kitchen didn't appreciate his acts of kindness. Some sneered at him, some spat at him and some yelled loudly at him if he tried to enforce the three sugar maximum in a cuppa tea. Some tried to punch him for reasons beyond rationalism and one guy pulled a knife on him when told that his syringes had been placed in safe keeping. Tim had found clean syringes after locking up the previous night and had given them to the local chemist. The chemist threw them out. When the patron called in at the kitchen to recover his syringes the next day, the knife came out and a wild street chase ensued that involved a bypass of the local police station. Police officers parking their vehicle spotted the armed patron as he ran past and joined the chase. Eventually the offender was tackled by one of the cops and handcuffed and Tim breathed a deep sigh of relief.

However the hardest thing was when regular patrons would scream at him because he wouldn't give them any money. He had helped one clean up his old flat and move all his stuff into a better flat and then up came the cash question. Tim never gave out cash because it would have been used on old habits that needed to die. The new resident started screaming at a distance of a few metres away and as Tim retreated the patron advanced more quickly. Soon the distance between them was reduced to a few centimetres. Face to face with a fist in reserve led to a silent prayer that seemed to get an answer. Tim had his back up to the kitchen wall and suddenly his attacker lowered his voice to a reasonable level and walked backwards apologizing. Tim was grateful it de-escalated but he still felt the weight of the rejection that had gone before.

Back at home the lounge, which had been left for them by the previous tenant, was replaced by a new three seater. Protests did not ensue. Tim also noticed that there were almost as many pot plants inside as there were trees outside. Lana had really set about improving the look of their home. She was pleased with her achievements but then her moods became less predictable and about five months into the marriage she started feeling unwell most mornings. The pregnancy test proved positive.

Tim was excited to hear the news but as he reflected on it, he wondered what sort of a father he was going to make. The black dog said he was going to be a lousy father and he struggled to envisage what it was going to look like. Both their workplaces were busy and they lost sight of each other as Lana fought for physical health and Tim fought for mental health. They still cared for each other but Lana relied more on her friends than Tim for most of the pregnancy. Tim retreated more into himself and Lana was confronted with the reality of his down times when he barely spoke to her.

One positive in the pregnancy was that both never missed a prenatal class. Tim sucked up all the info they gave as they outlined all the things that could go wrong. Lana felt his real love for her as they spoke about how to best handle the birth. The Birthing Centre at King George was the place that allowed the father to be fully present and even had a spa bath for slow birthing processes. Mums suffering infrequent contractions could support body weight in the water and dads could jump in to help. Tim envisaged himself in the spa on the big day but it was to be a fantasy that remained so. When Lana started getting contractions the first three were fast and furious. The rest periods in between were brief but Tim thought they would slow down. "It's only three contractions so far Lana – we have to wait and see how they average out before we go to the hospital."

"But they are so close together Tim."

"I'll pack my swimmers just in case it slows down a bit."

"The doctor said if the contractions aren't … aaahhh-hhnother one!!" Lana couldn't finish her sentence before another massive contraction took over but Tim had played footy and he still thought it wasn't bad enough to change plans. He informed Lana, "I'll be back in …" Then Lana screamed, "Forget the swimmers, ring the doctor!"

Something in the wild-eyed look of his wife convinced him to ring. "Hello doctor, Lana is having contractions one or two minutes apart …" The doctor then screamed on the phone, "Get her to the hospital now!" Their child was in a hurry to get out and Tim finally launched into action as though he was on the footy field.

When they arrived at King George a nurse screamed

at them, "Why did you wait so long!" With all the screaming Tim wasn't sure if he was on the field or in the soup kitchen but he whipped back at her, "The contractions only began half an hour ago." Lana was whipped away to the Birthing Centre, where two midwives attended to her and reassured her everything was going to be OK. She was in great pain and as Tim held her hand she squeezed so hard she almost broke a finger or two. Giving birth is still a life and death experience and Tim found himself praying for his wife and child. Screams more terrifying than the darkest Hollywood monsters came out of his wife's mouth and he kept hoping for the best.

Just two hours after the commencement of contractions a healthy son emerged, much to the relief of his mother but also to the wonder of his father. Tim was struck dumb with awe. He was so beautiful and he was theirs. An angelic cherub entered the world and his mother quickly recovered herself to hug him tightly with joy and wonder. It was a magic moment and Tim felt an incredible surge of love for his wife and son. Their child had come prepackaged with a download of love that seemed to surround him constantly. Before this revelation Tim had always considered newborns miniature Winston Churchills. How wrong he had been. The sight of little Matty breastfeeding in mum's embrace was more beautiful than any of the Seven Wonders of the Ancient World.

Matthew had been in a hurry to see the world but his escape plan had slowed down long enough to reduce the damage. Lana suffered a tear that should have been easily fixed but the doctor sewing up had been imprecise. She had to sit on a rubber pillow for a couple of weeks and was quite ginger about sitting down for much longer. However it was amazing how quickly she forgot the extreme pain she had endured at the time of birth. They were captivated by love for their son and they sure needed it when the challenges of parenting began to add up and appeared to be taking up more space than the rewards. Matty was taking over their lives.

Lana breastfed frequently and little Matty was becoming big Matty. Their boy had always been a big baby but they had been so besotted with his presence they hadn't really noticed his size compared to other babies. A Samoan friend commented he was as big as one of theirs. The matron of the hospital had warned Lana, "Lady you need to limit his feeding times or else you will have to wear him around like a broach." Matty had a big appetite and as he grew in size so Lana began to shrink. It wasn't just her post pregnancy belly that shrank. Her entire frame became thinner as bubba devoured her breast milk and her body fat too. Matthew hadn't yet learnt the law of diminishing returns, perhaps he never would. He just guzzled up milk as if he was at an all-you-can-eat buffet.

Bubba slept well but the night feeding sessions and constant attention newborns require was wearing Lana out. Tim took on the cooking when he got home from work and would change nappies whenever he was home. He also soaked and rinsed the cloth nappies. He took Matthew out in the pram day or night to help him get back to sleep and exhibited him to other parents at the local park. The long hours of parenting didn't allow any time off and Tim started to run low on energy too, as his sleep was interrupted by the changing routines of a young one. Tim refused to stop his volunteer work at the soup kitchen despite Lana's repeated requests.

Tim's parents came to visit their latest grandson and Tim was shocked to see how old his mother had become. It was a visit in which Bill planned to kill two birds with one stone. Liz wanted to see her grandson before it was too late. Her cancer had returned and Bill told his son quietly that she may only have weeks left. It was like Albert all over again. Tim thought, *"Why do you have to play everything so close to your chests?"* Tim had to withhold his temper from exploding there and then. He was not close to his parents emotionally but he did care about them despite his childhood regrets. Again he thought what he couldn't say, *"Why can't I talk to you like I can talk to Lana?"* Bill and Liz continued in small talk over afternoon tea, then grandpa and grandma left, after giving especially big hugs with their youngest son. A month later Bill called Tim after he had just placed a load of nappies in the washing machine. Liz had passed on. They didn't say much more than that before the phone call was over.

Wests weren't supposed to cry at funerals but Tim

broke the rule. He was grieving over his mother's death but also weeping with relief that he no longer attended these Catholic rituals, which only seemed to suck the life out of him. He pondered his mother and his life in her home and could feel the black dog creeping up on him. Work was super busy and the unending work at home was taking its toll on him. Lana could see he needed help and contacted her mum to come and give them a hand. Tim's mother-in-law was a quiet achiever who was happy to help as long as required. She was the complete opposite of the anagram mother-in-law (woman hitler!)

In the meantime Peggy had been telling Lana about an upcoming conference. It was an exploration of different spiritual beliefs that didn't promise it had all the answers but was prepared to keep asking questions. They had been interested in going but Lana thought it might be better if Tim went on his own. With her mum here helping, it would give Tim the break he needed. She put it to him, "I've noticed you are quite tired at the moment Tim."

"Yeah I'm about as tired as you my love."

"I asked mum to help because we are both tired but I also thought you could use a rest while she's here."

"What sort of rest?"

"Getting out of the home for a few days, maybe even going to a conference."

"Conferences are not a rest time but getting out sounds good."

"It's not your average conference. They talk in the morning, the afternoon is free and the nights are flexible."

"So it's not just a talk fest?"

"No, it's called Illusion, Delusion or Spiritual Reality."

"Hmm, sounds half interesting. I'll think about it."

"Don't think too hard, just entertain the possibility in your heart."

"OK, into the heart it goes, I guess."

"It starts in a week's time babe."

And so it was that Tim was destined to attend a conference that was going to be more than just a conference. It would provide what advertisers always promised but hardly ever delivered, a life-changing experience.

# REVELATION OF LOVE

## *Ultimate education*

~

Tim packed his bags for the live-in conference with a fairly heavy heart. He was glad to be a dad but had to juggle so many things, still not sure who he was or what he should be doing. He was a graphic designer, a husband, a father, a footballer, a social worker, a brother, a seeker, a victim, a whatever. How did he all fit together? His years of seeking truth had not satisfied his soul and he wondered if he could cope with any more new ideas at this open-ended conference.

The first session informed attendees to remain open-minded. Tim was not reassured by the possibility of more questions than he could handle. The second session was more promising. It focused on acceptance of 'the self' just as you are. There were no law-keeping requirements or heaven climbing responsibilities, rather just accept yourself in your current state. He spent the afternoon walking in a nearby woodland considering the wonders of nature, listening to the magpies and spotting a young wallaby in the scrub. He pondered the incredible gift that his son was to him 'just as he was'. Matthew hadn't done anything other than eat and excrete. It even occurred to Tim that he was once like Matthew, an adorable bundle of young flesh and bone, one who did not look like Winston Churchill.

The night session outlined various world views without specifying one was right, but rather showing that life is a journey in which world views are formed and reformed over and over. It was freeing for Tim to sense that he had journeyed a long way already, discounting extreme Catholic views and extreme humanist views, and he still had a long time to discover more possibilities without having to tick other people's boxes.

The next day considered various faith perspectives with time for questions and for meditation. The final session on Sunday afternoon looked at how bitterness can become a heavy load in life. Stories of Jews forgiving their Nazi jailers inspired a time of invitation in which participants were encouraged to come forward. It was a time for just you and God. Perhaps one might ask for the ability to forgive those who have hurt you. It was a last chance to do spiritual business before returning to the outside world where the focus on action squeezes out contemplation.

Tim immediately thought of a long-term patron, who had lashed out at Tim and then taken off to another city.

He hadn't thought of him since his departure because Tim had pushed the memory of this supposed friend to the back of his mind. The guy really had had a tough life as a young orphan passed around institutions like a gift no one wants. He thought of his own parents and how they likely did the best they could with what they had. Tim went forward as other people went forward. It was a physical sign of what he wanted to take place spiritually – to leave his hatred and unforgiveness behind and to walk away from the darkness. The woman leading the meeting was gently speaking about opening up hearts to receive what God is doing, when something happened to Tim.

Witnesses later told him that he fell backwards to the floor so fast onlookers were initially concerned that he had hurt himself. This surprised Tim greatly because he experienced it very differently. He did feel himself falling backwards but not in any fast way. Pairs of soft hands were holding him as he fell so it was like a slow motion movie in which he was falling into arms of love. The tenderness of the hands, the caress of his soul, the softness and warmth of the environment all rolled into an experience of supreme comfort, wonder and awe. As the hands faded Tim was surrounded by what felt like powder puff cushions, such was the gentleness of their touch. Then he felt he was floating and the light was easy on his eyes like reflections of candlelight in a romantic dinner. It was the most comfortable place Tim had ever experienced in his life and it just kept going on and on like he had crossed a barrier in the realm of timelessness where love reigns.

But then just as he felt the bliss would last forever, another force came into play. Darkness descended and Tim writhed in some small degree of pain. It struck a number of times but each time it came, the light drove it away and comfort was restored to his inner being. It was a struggle but one in which the outcome was not in doubt.

By the time Tim aroused from this magical state the auditorium was almost empty. The only group of people left, were those who had been looking after him while the struggle had been going on. The session leader was there as well as the few folk Tim had got to know over the weekend. Tim just smiled at them unaware of the strength of the battle that had just taken place. All he could feel was the ongoing warmth of the special place he had just visited. He was like a happy drunk, not able to stand up without assistance, and bursting into laughter without anyone telling a joke. The leader reassured everyone that he was OK though she was unsure of exactly what had transpired. All she knew was that it was very good.

One of the new friends offered to drop Tim at home because he was incapable of driving himself. It was a raucous journey home with much joy and laughter and Lana saw that the conference had done a great work on her husband even though he was incapable of walking unattended for a couple of days.

When Tim stopped laughing, he was able to declare to Lana, "I belong on the earth! The earth belongs to me!" Lana responded, "Hey babe of course you do," but she could see that there was more than just words happening here. Tim had always felt rejected in his heart by his parents, by his siblings, by his teachers, by the world at large, even though some people liked and even loved him. Now he was laughing away those rejections and he knew in the core of his being that he belonged here. The black dog had been driven out in this experience and Tim became so much more confident in himself and what he was to do in life.

It was no accident that Liz became pregnant with a fifth son, Tim knew his conception had come from God. His mother's initial rejection had been fully displaced by the love of God. The misdirected pin in hospital, which had given him a fear of needles, no longer had power over any part of him. Ongoing feelings of abandonment lessened and were no longer fed by the desertion of Luke, his next door neighbour and almost best friend. And unlike his convict ancestors, Tim no longer felt rejected by his ancient homeland; he knew Australia was his home as much as it was his indigenous brothers.

When he saw his father the following week, he was still in the thrall of his love awakening and Bill noticed that Tim was full of affection for the whole family. Why he even hugged Harold for longer than was really necessary. Harold remembered for a moment the occasional affection he had for Tim as a baby but he could only respond via an Aussie pat on the back. Bill received his embrace whole heartedly and hugged back as the memory of their time in the principal's office came back to him.

When Tim's friends saw him after 'the event' as it became known among them, they were similarly surprised by his unashamed displays of affection. Hugs between the boys were often tests of who could produce the strongest bearhug in the literal sense of the term. But Sam and even more surprisingly Mitch, found themselves unable to squeeze hard when Tim was the opponent. Rather they would begin to melt a bit as something other worldly came into the room. Perhaps more than a little love transference was taking place between the boys.

Peggy was in raptures about what had happened to Tim at the conference. Most of what she thought about the event was shared with Lana in private but she was the one person who was able to hug Tim back with the same amount of enthusiasm his wife did.

Laughter now became a regular part of Tim's life and not just when he was watching shows like "Who's Line is it Anyway?" He was able to laugh in the face of adversity in a way that defied the logic of the circumstances and saved him from allowing black clouds to settle on his spirit. Matty loved his dad's laughter and would always join in triumphantly and if Lana was in hearing distance, a rolling session could well develop with all three of them bumping into one another. Not many understood why Tim could laugh in the absence of any obvious comedic activity but the people who mattered to him most understood. They knew his feet had been firmly established on a love foundation by the one who made them all in the first place.

Healing a heart is however not a one week job nor a one year job. It takes real time and the measure of it can vary considerably from one individual to another. The scorn of teachers like Decimus lay etched on the deeper layers of Tim's heart ... deep, deep down. The pain of his mother's abuse was hidden further beneath multiple layers of protection yet somehow he knew that he had not been a victim of sexual abuse like his Year Five colleagues. He had suffered the same sort of emotional manipulation that held boys like him captive to lies. Intuitively he saw before him the five faces of classmates who had undergone private investigations of their supposedly private parts. Tim felt compassion for these abused souls and hoped God would reveal the same love he was feeling towards them as well.

The crimes of the Marist order would one day be exposed and be set right in a small way. There would come a day in court in which Decimus was found guilty of most of the crimes he had been charged with. Sadly the five plaintiffs didn't have the satisfaction of the jury upholding the most serious violations. How many abusers, whether Catholic or other, have also escaped the full extent of the law? The world is simply not a place where fair is fair. Though his friends were still held captive, Tim felt as though all his chains had been cut through. The sense of freedom he was experiencing was full and he felt like he might live forever.

He loved Lana with a renewed passion and he was able to more easily forgive people who hurt him. He stopped his volunteering for a time to enable him time to become a better husband and father. He knew God was real and that God was good. Questions remained about the injustices of the world but the certainty of God's goodness and His concern for Tim was etched into his heart. Just like Lana had said, God does care about Tim and about his family and about everyone on the planet too he guessed.

God had met him in the place where he most needed it and such a foundation would not be washed away. It was fastened to the ground of his soul and whatever else might happen in life he knew that God was there to help. Tim West belongs on the earth. God made him **and still loves him** with a passion that will never die.

# AFTERWORD

This account is fictional but truth underlies the greater part of it. The only stories guaranteed not to have suffered from exaggeration are the spiritual ones. We humans don't often feel the love that Tim experienced but it exists more closely to our hearts than we've been led to believe. Nothing will ultimately undermine the reality of God's love for us and for all creation and that ultimately includes you the reader. Many thanks for coming this far with me.

# ACKNOWLEDGEMENTS

William Paul Young's book, 'The Shack' and Trent Dalton's, 'Boy Swallows Universe' were major inspirations in helping me recognise the power of real stories in fictional settings. U2 are my favourite band and their communication of love, hope and peace helped inspire me to place LOVE at the top of my priorities in life. Love has come into town and it ain't leaving baby.

Early on my daughter Charlotte was the first person to read the opening chapters and she encouraged me to keep writing because it was good. Thanks to editor Sonia Naea and husband Frank who helped me believe my first novel is one of quality. Marg Auty, my wife Lynne and others also helped me understand I needed to rewrite or reconsider parts of it and it is the better for it. It really is a work of fiction based on many real events and people but with just as many layers of invention.

# DISCLAIMER

For those who know the author personally this is a work of fiction. Composite characters and events abound. Liz, Bill, Harold, Sam, Mitch and Lana do not exist but have been inspired by various people and events, as well as the need for dramatic exaggeration in a novel such as this. James played for NSW but not Australia. He has been to Central Asia but not Sikkim and so on. Something happened to him before school but he has no clear memory of it. He is grateful to all his family and friends for the love and support they have freely given to him over the years and he looks forward to reconnecting with his mum and dad in the next life.

www.ingramcontent.com/pod-product-compliance
Lightning Source LLC
Chambersburg PA
CBHW011933050726

47590CB00011B/3269